Object Oriented Programming Using C++

An Introduction

John Pardoe and Melv King

First published 1997 by
MACMILLAN PRESS LTD
Houndmills, Basingstoke, Hampshire RG21 6XS
and London
Companies and representatives
throughout the world

ISBN 0–333–69241–1

A catalogue record for this book is available
from the British Library.

This book is printed on paper suitable
for recycling and made from fully
managed and sustained forest sources.

10 9 8 7 6 5 4 3 2 1
06 05 04 03 02 01 00 99 98 97

Printed and bound in Great Britain by
Antony Rowe Ltd, Chippenham, Wiltshire

Contents

Preface

Aim of the book

The increasing use of object oriented techniques for software development is now a fact of life.

- Increasingly large software projects must use object oriented techniques.
- It has been predicted that object oriented programming will provide the focus for all new software development.
- The concepts of software reuse are becoming increasingly important.

The aim of this book is to provide an introductory course in the use of object oriented computer programming using the C++ language. It has been especially designed to teach those with no previous experience of computer programming.

Many student programmers learn more traditional, procedural approaches to computer programming before tackling the quite different concepts found in object oriented programming; many students find this switch difficult. Hence the need for an introductory text that encourages students to understand basic programming concepts and techniques within an object oriented framework.

Other books in this area have tended to incorporate so much material, much of it difficult to assimilate, that the novice reader could well be discouraged. The temptation to include too much has therefore been resisted. Complex terminology has been eliminated or explained in simple terms.

What we have included are the basic concepts and terminology of object oriented programming that will enable the reader to 'get started' and build up the confidence to move on to more advanced texts.

Content of the book

The book develops the techniques of object oriented programming at the same time as gradually introducing the language features of C++. Procedural aspects that should be included in any introductory text, such as the use of structured programming techniques, have been incorporated.

Many straightforward examples are used to introduce and illustrate both new techniques and language features.

Chapter 1 covers basic concepts in order that the reader can appreciate what a computer program is. The development of a program is then put in context by describing briefly, in general terms, the various stages involved. Chapter 2 introduces the basic object oriented terminology and illustrates how object classes are used to model a very simple system.

Having introduced a C++ program in chapter 3, the important concept of inheritance and the use of a header file are covered in chapter 4.

Chapters 5 to 8 cover, within an object oriented context, facilities found in most procedural languages, such as basic data types, arithmetic and control constructs for selection and repetition. The need for, and the difference between, the constructs for both selection and repetition are emphasised.

Chapter 9 concentrates on the use of programmer-defined functions; concepts are introduced by referring to functions already used including those found in standard C++ libraries. The next chapter on the use of constructors and destructors is a natural development.

The need for arrays and their use is described in chapters 11 to 13. The concept of an array of objects enables the difference between inheritance and aggregation to be explained.

Scope rules and object lifetime are emphasised in chapter 14 before introducing the concept of pointers for dynamic variables and objects. Then chapter 15 covers the use of file streams in general and how they may be used to facilitate object persistence.

Finally, in chapter 16, we introduce some of the fundamental concepts of polymorphism and use appropriate C++ language constructs in straightforward illustrative examples.

Use of the book

Each chapter starts with the learning objectives for the chapter and concludes with a number of exercises. The chapters have been kept relatively short so that the reader can use the exercises to ensure that concepts are understood and techniques mastered in accordance with the objectives.

There are two types of exercise. The first type is a self-assessment question designed to reinforce major points by referring the reader back to specific examples in the chapter. The second type of exercise involves either amending one or more of the example programs or writing a new program. The reader is strongly advised to attempt all the exercises and for the second type to run the program and get it working. Sample solutions to all the exercises are given in appendix B.

An outline design, indicating how each function achieves a specific task, is provided in most of the examples and all the practical exercises; it is written in a form of structured English (pseudo-code). This emphasises to the reader the importance of understanding 'how to solve the problem' before 'coding in C++'. It also demonstrates how to write pseudo-code and provides appropriate help for the novice when attempting the practical exercises.

A model and corresponding object class for a student's performance (examination and practical mark) in a subject (module) is introduced in a simplified form in chapter 5. This model is developed and refined in subsequent chapters as additional features of object oriented programming are introduced. This case study approach promotes the learning process as well as providing an awareness of the reality of software systems development using object oriented programming. A diagram showing all the object classes that are eventually used and the relationship between them is given in appendix A. This diagram also indicates where each class is first introduced in the text enabling the reader to refer back, if necessary, for the full specification.

Acknowledgement

The authors are grateful to Neil Hepworth of South Bank University for his helpful and constructive comments made while reviewing this book.

1   Programming Concepts

Objectives for this chapter
Familiarity with the programming terms:
- identifier, data type
- integer, float, character and string
- constants and variables
- source code and coding
- compiler, compilation, syntax errors
- program execution, run-time errors, logical errors
- testing, test data, bugs, debugging
- user requirements specification, program design, documentation and maintenance
- sequence, iteration and selection constructs
- program characteristics: correctness, reliability, modifiability and clarity.

Understanding of:
- how the computer and the programmer identify data items
- how values may be given to data items
- how data are accepted and displayed.

1.1 Computer programs

A computer program is a sequence of instructions, often a very long sequence, that can be held in a computer's internal storage area (memory) and executed at speed. The instructions are normally first written down in a human-readable form, called the **source code** or **program code**, and entered into the computer's memory or a computer file via the keyboard. The source code is written using a **high-level programming language**, such as Pascal, C, C++, Ada, COBOL. Instructions, written in these languages are referred to as **program statements**. This source code has to be translated into a form that can be understood by the electronics of the computer; this is known as the **machine code** and the translation process is called **compilation**.

A computer program will normally take some data values, store the data in memory and then manipulate the values to produce the required results. For example, a simple program might take in ten temperature readings in degrees

Fahrenheit and convert them to degrees Celsius. A more complex program for a company's payroll system would take in a great deal of data, staff names, tax codes, salary grades and so on, in order to produce results in the form of payslips and cheques or bank credits. The values that the program takes in are known generally as the **input data** and the results are often referred to as the **output**. This can be visualised as in figure 1.1.

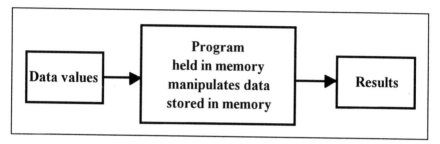

Figure 1.1

1.2 The way a program uses the computer's memory

Within the computer itself, each unit of memory (called a **byte**) is accessed or **addressed** by a unique reference number. In some cases a single byte is addressed, in others two or more bytes are addressed as if they are one complete unit of memory.

To make programs more readable, however, the programmer refers to parts of the computer's memory by an identifying name, called an **identifier**. Since different types of data are stored differently, we also need the concept of a **data type**. The standard data types used in most computer programming languages are: **integer, float** (or real), **character**, and **string**. An integer item is restricted so that it will contain only whole numbers within a pre-specified range, for example in the range -32,768 to +32,767. Data of type float is for real numbers, that is numbers that may contain a decimal part. While integer and float data items use more than one byte, an item of type character uses only one byte and is restricted to contain just one character. The character may be any that is recognised by the computer, including some special ones as well as the usual letters of the alphabet and numbers. Finally, a text string is a number of characters such as a person's name or the name of a product, stored in a succession of bytes.

We can illustrate the way in which the programmer and the computer access items of data by considering the diagram in figure 1.2.

If we imagine that the diagram represents a portion of the computer's memory and that each cell is one byte, we can give a unique numerical reference to each byte by using the column and row numbers. Hence the cell at the top left-hand corner containing the letter B is referred to as byte 00, the one to its right as byte 01 and the one directly beneath it as byte 10, and so on.

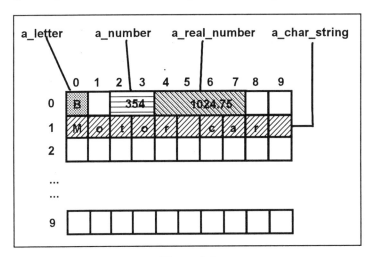

Figure 1.2

Within a program, all we have to do is specify (or **declare**) the names of the identifiers (in this case, **a_letter**, **a_number**, **a_real_number** and **a_char_string**) and state which data type they are to contain (**character**, **integer**, **float**, **string**), the computer references and in most cases the number of bytes to be used are calculated during the compilation process.

Areas of computer memory reserved to hold data in a computer program may have initial values (or **constant values**) pre-loaded into them automatically when the program is first run, or values may be **assigned** to the areas during the running of the program. This is illustrated in figure 1.3.

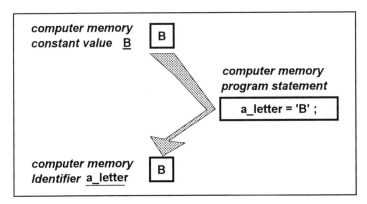

Figure 1.3

In this diagram, we have three areas of computer memory. At the top we have a single byte that is of data type character and it contains the constant value B that it will retain for the duration of the program. Not surprisingly, we call this kind of data **constant** data. At the bottom of the diagram, we have also a single byte that has been given the identifying name **a_letter** and the data type character. Because **a_letter** may be given any value during the running of a computer program it is referred to as a **variable identifier** (or just **variable** for short). The third area of memory shown is that which is needed to hold a computer instruction written in the C++ language to change the value of the identifier so that it contains the letter B; we call this kind of instruction an assignment statement, it is one way of changing the values held in a computer program's memory. Another way is depicted in figure 1.4.

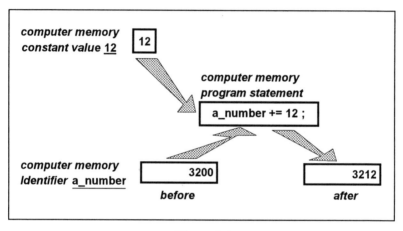

Figure 1.4

Here the computer instruction shown, again in the C++ language, is one that adds a fixed value (the constant number 12) to the existing contents of the variable identifier **a_number** giving it a new value. Again, three areas of memory are shown; the two data areas would be integers.

The above examples use elementary data types containing a single item of data. Groups of data items may also be declared using a single identifier. The components of these groups may all be of the same type or of a number of different types.

1.3 Input and output of data

As mentioned in section 1.1, a program will normally take in some input values and produce results known as output.

The input values can be held in computer **files** on disk or typed at the keyboard. In either case, the data are first stored in a small area of memory called a **buffer**. When a computer program issues an instruction to **read** or **accept** the data, the required value(s) are transferred into memory areas within

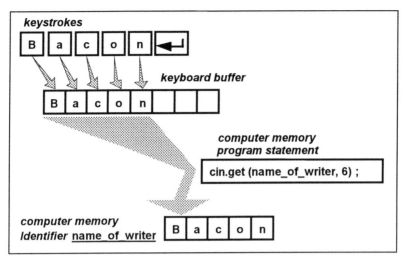

Figure 1.5

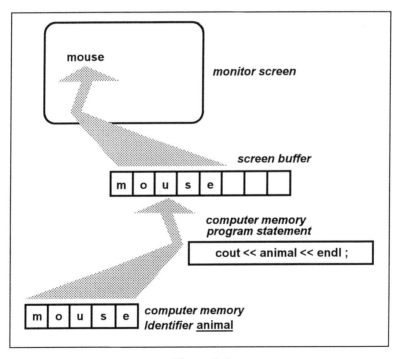

Figure 1.6

the program. This general process for keyboard input is shown in figure 1.5. The program statement illustrated here is written in the C++ language.

Note that the programmer generally does not need to be concerned with the buffer.

The process of producing output is almost the reverse of obtaining input data. **Writing** data to a disk file and **displaying** data on the monitor screen also involves a memory buffer that we do not need to concern ourselves with unduly. For such output activities, we need to do two things: identify the memory area from which the data will be taken and indicate where the output is to be placed; the name of the computer file and in some cases the position in the file or the position on the screen where the data are to be displayed. The general process for displaying just one item on the screen is depicted in figure 1.6. Again, the program statement is written in the C++ language.

1.4 Computer program development

The stages of computer program development are most often referred to as the software life-cycle. A number of different models have been produced to describe this life-cycle with the major differences being the breakdown of the different stages and the way certain stages may be repeated or occur concurrently.

In the following sections we describe the stages separately, but it should be understood that the stages may overlap and that it may be necessary to return to a previous stage. For example, the testing stage if not completed to the developer's satisfaction could require adjustments at the programming stage.

A life-cycle model can be applied to a single computer program or a collection of programs that make up a complete computer system.

1.5 The user requirements specification

The user requirements specification is normally a document that describes in precise terms what is required of a computer program (or computer system). It is produced after an analysis process in which systems analysts consult with the probable eventual users of the system to explore the current and future requirements in a specific business or technical area. It will be concerned with what will actually be delivered to the users at the end of the development process or each development stage.

The user requirements specification is the result of a refining process whereby general statements of desire or intent to produce a computer system are formalised; it becomes the foundation for the system's development. An analysis process (called object oriented analysis or OOA) will define the components (objects) of the real world that are to be modelled in the proposed computer system. This will focus on the information that is required to be processed as well as the functional requirements (specific activities).

The details of how the information needs of the system are to be met or how the specific requirements are to be provided are not produced at this stage.

1.6 The design stages

The design stages translate the user requirements into a representation of the proposed system that can be assessed for quality and can facilitate the production of computer program code.

The systems design stage is concerned with all aspects of the system, not just the production of computer programs. For example, the design of clerical procedures and management of the system would need detailed consideration as well as what the computer software is to achieve.

The software design stage is concerned with how the real-world objects identified in the analysis stage are to be represented in the computer system and how they may interact.

This will include how and where data are to be stored within computer files or in computer memory during the running of computer programs. It will involve the determination of what data are to be grouped together and what types of data storage are needed for storing different kinds of values.

It will also include a definition of the relationship between the major components of the system (or program) and design representations of the detailed processes that the system requires.

1.7 Detailed design using pseudo-code

As we shall see in the next chapter, a large program is normally broken down into self-contained parts called **functions**. Each function consists of the steps required to achieve a specific task; eventually it will be written in program statements using the appropriate programming language. First, at this stage, the tasks are written in an informal notation called **pseudo-code**.

Pseudo-code contains normal language statements to describe the actions required and also more formalised control statements to indicate the logic. For example, the normal language statements for the C++ statements shown in figures 1.3 to 1.6 are:

```
Assign 'B' to a_letter
Add 12 to a_number
Accept name of writer (from keyboard)
Display animal (on monitor screen)
```

Control statements are similar to C++ statements and will be described in detail in the appropriate chapters.

We can describe the logic of most functions using the three constructs: **sequences**, **iterations** and **selections**.

A **sequence** is a number of statements that will be executed in the order written from top to bottom of the paper.

An **iteration** is the repetition of one or more statements.

A **selection** is a choice between two or more different actions depending on the value of a data item or some other condition.

1.8 The programming stage

Writing computer programs involves far more than just learning a programming language; it is very easy to write poor programs. Problems that we are trying to solve by computer must be carefully defined. Then when the definition or **specification** is clearly understood, we can design a solution to the problem using pseudo-code. Only after the design process is complete should we elaborate the design by producing programming language statements (or program code) from it. This is known as the **coding** process or implementing the design.

1.9 Compiling, running and testing a program

As mentioned in section 1.1, a source program cannot be understood directly by the computer; it must first be translated into an equivalent program in the machine language (code) of the computer.

This process of translation (compilation), is performed by a program stored within the computer called a **compiler**. This produces a machine-readable form of the program that is combined with code from the **compiler libraries** using a process called **linking**. This two-stage process produces a machine language program that is then stored either in a disk file or in computer memory, but it will only do this if there are no mistakes in the way you have used the language. If there are **syntax errors**, that is, mistakes in the program language grammar, then the compiler will produce **error messages**.

Once we have produced a program without syntax errors and have a machine language program in computer storage, we can go to the next stage, **execution**. The computer executes the machine code instructions and may produce the results you require. However, at this stage further errors can occur. **Run-time** (or execution) errors occur when the programmer has made a mistake that was not a syntax error, but still contravenes the computer's rules (for example, trying to divide a number by zero). In such cases an appropriate **run-time error** message is produced.

Logical errors occur even when there are no syntax or run-time errors. The symptoms for these errors are results that are not as expected. The design may be wrong or they may arise because the programming language statements are misused or in the wrong order.

The error messages will help us to find the syntax and run-time errors. Detecting logical errors can obviously be more difficult. It is vitally important that we **test** our program, possibly with a range of data values, known as **test data**, to ensure that it works according to its specification. The task of finding out why a program is not working to specification is called **debugging**. This is because logical errors in programs are called **bugs**. If we discover that the program is not correct for any reason, then we must change the contents of the source program.

1.10 Documenting and maintaining programs

Documentation is that information concerning a program that is needed by both users of the program and those with responsibility for maintaining the program. The former need sufficient detail to enable them to use the program properly. The latter need sufficient detail to enable them to modify, improve and correct the program.

Good **user documentation** is essential if a program is to be a useful tool; an outstanding piece of software is useless if no one knows how to use it. The contents and style of a user guide will obviously vary depending on the target audience. For example, a user guide for a software tool that is to be used by experienced programmers will need almost no information about how to switch the computer system on. However, a user guide for the general public, such as a Windows 95 User Guide will need to contain instructions on how to turn on the computer and how to use disks.

Good **technical documentation** is essential for maintaining a program. We may have to correct errors or we may decide to add features and improve the program. Programs have actually been thrown away because they are too difficult to change. A technical manual should enable someone other than the author, but who is familiar with the design methods and documentation standards, to understand fully the program's purpose and the way that the purpose has been achieved.

When do we write this documentation? The rule is, document as you go along. Much of the user documentation should be written as we start to design a program, it can serve as a set of specifications. As we proceed with the development of a program, much of the technical documentation can be written. This should ensure that the documentation will be of a high quality. If documentation is left until the end of the project, important details are often omitted.

When the program is complete and full-scale testing has been done, the documentation should be reviewed to check that it meets its stated purpose and that it is accurate and consistent with the finished program.

Maintenance can be defined as "anything that happens to program code after the initial implementation". It can be classified into four areas: corrective maintenance, adaptive maintenance, perfective maintenance and preventive maintenance.

The most obvious form of maintenance is error fixing or **corrective maintenance**. Here we concern ourselves with removing a known fault from a program or system.

Adaptive maintenance is the act of modifying a software unit so that it interfaces with a changing environment. It commonly occurs when changes in hardware, the operating system or other system software force alterations to be made to application programs.

Perfective maintenance is the most common type of maintenance encompassing enhancements both to the function and the efficiency of the code.

It usually arises from requests for change to the user requirements specification.

Preventive maintenance is the process of changing software to improve its future maintainability or to provide a better basis for future enhancements.

1.11 Writing high-quality computer programs

Writing computer programs is both exciting and creative. It also needs discipline and a systematic approach if the desired results are to be achieved. This is because there may be many ways of writing a computer program but not all of them will lead to the production of a program of the required quality.

To produce high-quality programs, we need to be aware of the four basic criteria for quality. They are: correctness, reliability, modifiability and clarity.

Correctness is obviously an essential quality in that we would always wish to ensure that a computer program does what it is supposed to do in the most appropriate manner. It must satisfy its requirements or specification in all aspects.

A computer program must also be reliable in that it will always produce predictable results every time it is run. Most computer programs will operate on different sets of data each time they are run hence there may be many different results to be produced.

Of increasing importance as a requirement of high-quality software is modifiability. Most computer programs will require some modification, or maintenance, at some time because the requirements of the program may change or better techniques are discovered or even to correct residual errors.

To be modifiable a computer program must be easy to understand. Hence clarity is an essential characteristic of high-quality programs. It is easy to produce over-complex programs. However, it should be noted that bad programmers produce unnecessarily complicated programs; good programmers only ever produce simple, clearly understood programs.

Our goal should be to provide high-quality programs using a method of proceeding from a statement of the program's requirements to high-quality solution in a reasonable manner. Object oriented design and programming is a means of achieving this.

1.12 Exercises

1.12.1   State in your own words what is meant by the following terms:
    (a) Compilation of a computer program.
    (b) Identifier.
    (c) Data type.
    (d) Variable.
    (e) Keyboard buffer.

1.12.2 Answer the following questions:
  (a) How does a computer programmer identify a particular part of the memory in a computer program? .
  (b) What different kinds of data might you wish to use in a computer program?
  (c) What is an assignment statement?

1.12.3 State in your own words what is meant by the following terms:
  (a) The user requirements specification.
  (b) Pseudo-code.
  (c) Testing.
  (d) The reliability of a computer program.

1.12.4 Answer the following questions:
  (a) Why is the software life-cycle not a strictly sequential set of development stages?
  (b) What type of errors may be discovered when compiling and then testing a computer program?
  (c) What is the process of fault diagnosis more commonly called?
  (d) What is the difference between user-documentation and technical documentation?
  (e) What are the four types of program or system maintenance?
  (f) Why are simplicity and clarity necessary requisites of a good computer program?

2 Object Oriented Programming Concepts

Objectives for this chapter
Familiarity with the object oriented terms:
- object and object class
- object class data, object class behaviour and functions
- an instance of an object class
- inheritance, base class, derived class
- encapsulation
- private and public parts of an object class
- polymorphism.

Ability to:
- draw a diagram to represent a simple object class
- draw a diagram to illustrate inheritance of an object class
- model a simple object class in terms of its data items and behaviour (functions).

2.1 Concept of a model

Computer programs **model** or **simulate** real-world or imaginary-world objects and their interactions. We can illustrate this by considering a simple computer game in which the user guides a little figure around a maze. The little figure is a model of a person who can walk around a maze. As with all models, because they are models, they do not have all of the facilities of their real-world counterparts. Our little figure may only be required to "walk" in each of the four compass directions (because the walls of the maze are at right angles to each other), and "recognise" when it reaches a wall, and "decide" which direction to take next. Note that the verbs "walk", "recognise" and "decide" describe the **behaviour** or the **functions** of the model. Other aspects of the model might be its colour and the size of the figure. These attributes are information (or **data**) that describe the structure and nature of the model. They do not necessarily influence the behaviour of the model, but may do so, for example, if an aspect of the behaviour was a function to change the colour or size.

We can describe a real-world object in terms of its component parts (its

data) and what it does (its **behaviour**). When we produce a model of such an object, we decide which features we are going to use in the model. First we look at the component parts and choose what we need in our model; we may ask ourselves "Which of the component parts of the object are important in our simulation?" Next, we choose those functions of the behaviour of the object that we wish to simulate.

In what sense do we produce a model or use simulation when developing a computer program? Clearly, it is not in the same sense as building a model of a person from clay or wood. Rather, we use pictures, words and numbers. We manipulate these in the computer to give some desired affect possibly on the monitor screen. For example, a model of a person in a computer would probably consist of graphical representations of a person in different poses as well as descriptive data in words concerning such things as the person's name and numerical data for such things as size.

So, the model's data can be described in terms of graphics, words and numbers, but what of the model's behaviour? Each aspect of the behaviour represents a function to be defined. For example, our little figure in the maze has a "walk" function. This would be quite a complicated function to implement; others in different simulations could be more straightforward. For instance, if we were to produce a computer function to simulate the withdrawal of money from a bank account, it might be just two simple calculations: subtract sum of money from account; and add sum of money to contents of wallet.

Object oriented programming emphasises the interconnections between data items and functional behaviour in a way that puts together information and processing rather than processing alone. An **object** is a component implemented in software such that it contains a definition of its data and the functions (operations) that describe the object's behaviour or how the data is used or interacts with its environment.

2.2 Object classes and objects

It would be very wasteful to describe uniquely each individual object as we need them because most objects tend to have some things (data or behaviour) in common with others. Often it is convenient to group objects together such as in the field of zoology in grouping animal species with common characteristics. Such groupings in programming are called **object classes**.

Object classes can be thought of as descriptions of categories or groups of objects. For example, the object class `car` may have a description pertaining to the relevant features that apply to all cars. All cars have wheels and an engine; they consume fuel and so on. The object class `employee` might have the general description of all people employed in a certain situation; and would likely comprise name, date of birth and current salary among other areas of interest.

We can apply what we have already seen when introducing the notion of models to object classes. What we know about the component parts of an object class is called the **member data** (or attributes). The member data for an employee could be `name`, `date of birth` and so on. The things we can do with an object class or its data are called its **behaviour**. For example, we can give an employee a pay rise or amend an employee's qualifications. The definition of the **member functions** that define an object's behaviour is part of an object class's description. Each function will normally consist of the actions required to achieve a specific task.

One way of describing the object class for an employee is by means of an object schema as given in figure 2.1.

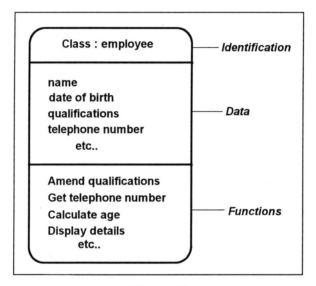

Figure 2.1

Notice how we identify the object data and the object behaviour (functions). In a full description, we would normally have one or more functions for each item of data. If we asked "What can we do with each item of data?", the answer would generate a list of functions. For example, if we asked this question of just one data item, say `telephone number`, we would likely generate: `insert new number`, `amend existing number`, `delete number`, `display full number`, `extract dialling code`, and perhaps many more.

An **object** is said to be an **instance** of an object class. This means that an object is an implementation of an object class definition. We can liken an object to a more complex version of a variable in a program; a variable has a type that describes its characteristics (for example, an integer is a whole number within a certain range); an object has an object class that describes its characteristics. For example, we might have objects `Jim_Brown` and `Dave_Thomas` of the object class **employee**.

Objects have all the data items and functions of their class. Hence, to change **Jim_Brown**'s qualifications, we would use the function **amend qualifications**. The object oriented terminology for this is that we "send a **message** to the object"; so we send the message **amend_qualifications** to **Jim_Brown**.

2.3 Inheritance

If we develop the example of the object class **employee**, it is easy to see that there are different kinds of employee all having a common set of characteristics as described in the definition of the object class **employee**. Also we can see that different kinds of employee would have additional, more specific, characteristics depending on their position or type of work. For example, an employee who is a manager might be responsible for a number of staff and may have a secretary (who can be described by name or perhaps employee number). We therefore need to use the attributes and behaviour from the original class and extend them to include the particular characteristics of each type of employee.

The concept of **inheritance** allows us to produce another class such that it has all the data and functions of the class upon which it is based (called the **base class**). The new class called a **derived class** can be thought of as a specialised version of the more general base class.

So, a class that **inherits** the data and behaviour of another is called a **derived class** often referred to as a **descendant** or a **child class**. The class that provides the inherited characteristics is called the **base class** also referred to as an **ancestor** or **parent** class.

The way in which a derived class is formed by inheritance from a base class is depicted in the object schema shown in figure 2.2.

An entire inheritance (or classification) hierarchy (like a family tree) may be constructed from a single class with a number of descendants. This is illustrated in figure 2.3 where the base class **employee** has three descendants: **manager**, **secretary** and **technician**. The **manager** derived class is also a base class with one descendant: **sales manager**.

Note that the inheritance of data and behaviour in a program is usually achieved by sharing the code and not duplicating it, so the inherited functions and data do not actually exist in the derived class. To illustrate this, imagine we wish to use the function **get telephone number** from the **manager** class, the computer would first look for the function in **manager**, then on failing to find it there it would look further up the class hierarchy until the function is found.

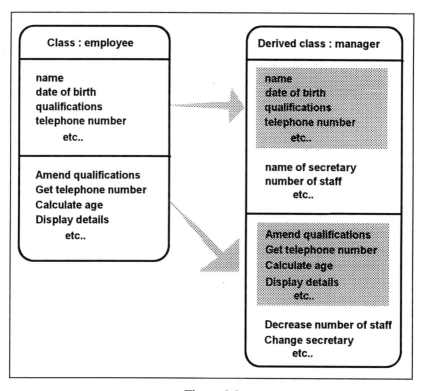

Figure 2.2

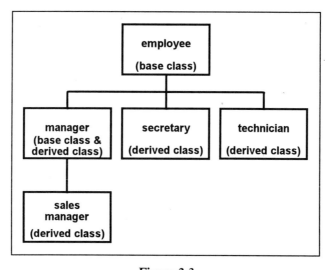

Figure 2.3

2.4 Encapsulation

Putting data and functions together is called **encapsulation**. A basic principle of object oriented programming is that member data should only be accessed via the object's own functions. To achieve this, in all but exceptional cases, member data items are described as **private** or **protected**. Functions may also be private. If data or functions are to be accessed directly from outside the object class, they are defined as **public**.

Encapsulation separates how an object class behaves from how it is implemented and therefore allows the details of an object class to be modified without requiring changes to applications that use the object class. The object class can be treated as a **black box**, the programmer needs only to know what functions can be requested and not how they are carried out.

2.5 Polymorphism

Polymorphism means having many forms. In object oriented programming it refers to the way in which different objects may respond to the same message in different ways depending on the type of the object. For example, `manager` and `technician` objects should respond differently to the `Display details` message. The functions need to be different even though the purpose of the function is the same, that is, to display the details of the object concerned.

There are a number of ways to implement polymorphism, we will discuss these later in the text.

2.6 Modelling a system using object classes

Suppose we wish to model the activities of a University; we could define an object class `person` with derived classes `student` and `tutor` and an object class `course`. To keep things simple, let us assume that these are the only objects of interest and their data items are as follows.

```
person:    name,
           reference number,
           year of joining the University.
student:   as for person,
           year of the course.
tutor:     as for person,
           years of teaching experience.
course:    name,
           number of students.
```

Again, to keep it simple, their functions are:

person:	**Initialise details:** to allow the entry of the three data items for a person.
	Display details: to display the values of all three data items of a person.
student:	**Initialise details:** to allow the entry of the three data items for a person, plus the year of the course.
	Display details: to display the values of all three data items of a person, plus the year of the course.
tutor:	**Initialise details:** to allow the entry of the three data items for a person, plus the years of teaching experience.
	Display details: to display the values of all three data items of a person, plus the years of teaching experience.
course:	**Initialise details:** to allow the entry of course name and setting the number of students to zero.
	Add new student: to use the student initialise details function and add one to the number of students.
	Display details: to display the course name followed by the number of students on the course.

We can represent the relationship between the object classes using an object schema similar to that shown in figure 2.2, as follows in figure 2.4. Note that, in this case, for the derived classes the functions are over-ridden (redefined) because they must be different for each class.

2.7 Exercises

2.7.1   State in your own words what is meant by the following object oriented terms:
(a) An object class.
(b) A function.
(c) An attribute.
(d) Inheritance.
(e) Encapsulation.

2.7.2   Answer the following questions:
(a) In what way is an object similar to a variable?
(b) What are two other names given to derived classes?
(c) What is a software "black box"?

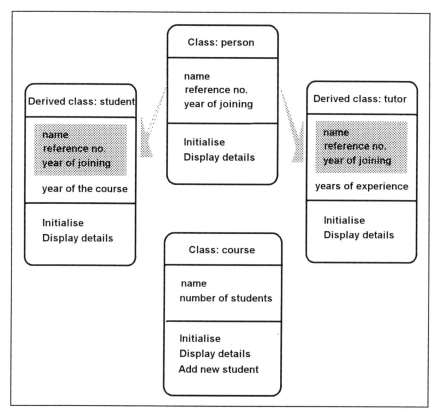

Figure 2.4

2.7.3 Please examine the object schema in figure 2.2 and answer the following questions.
   (a) What data members are inherited by the derived class **manager** from **employee**?
   (b) What other data members might the derived class **manager** have?
   (c) What other derived classes do you think might be derived from the class **employee**?

2.7.4 In a warehouse system, the following objects have been identified as having the data items:

```
container:   name,
             location,
             weight.
carton:      as for container,
             destination,
             number of components.
```

| `case:` | as for container,
`quality control reference.` |

The functions are:

`container:`	`Initialise details:` to allow the entry of the three data items for a container. `Display details:` to display the values of all three data items of a container.

`carton:`	`Initialise details:` to allow the entry of the three data items for a container, plus the destination and number of components.
	`Display details:` to display the values of all three data items of a container, plus the destination and number of components.
	`Amend the number of components.`
	`Amend the destination.`

`case:`	`Initialise details:` to allow the entry of the three data items for a container, plus the quality control reference. `Display details:` to display the values of all three data items of a container, plus the quality control reference.

Draw an object schema that shows the relationship between the class `container` and the derived classes `carton` and `case`.

3   A First Program

3.1 The model for our first program

Let us examine a simple program that displays a message on the monitor screen. We need an object class that defines the contents of the message and at least two functions. We need a function to give an initial value to the message and a function to display the contents of the message. With a little thought we could probably specify other functions such as determining the position on the screen or defining the colour of the background and foreground for the message. However, we will keep it simple and produce a model of the problem in the form of an object class with just two functions, as shown in the object schema given in figure 3.1.

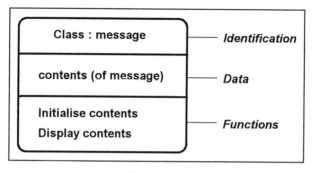

Figure 3.1

3.2 The C++ code for our first program

Figure 3.2 contains the complete C++ code to display a message. Please accept for the moment the necessity for what may appear to be many programming statements for a straightforward task. The benefits of this approach will only become apparent when we consider more complicated examples.

We will now explain this program line by line by repeating small parts of the code with an explanation of the component parts.

The first two lines in our program are comments.

```
// HELLO.CPP
// A program to display the Hello World message
```

A comment is introduced by the two consecutive characters //. Everything that follows on that line is considered to be explanatory text that does not affect the running of the program. Comments are ignored by the compiler and are included to explain the program to a human reader. They can be placed anywhere in a program, on lines by themselves as above, or towards the end of a line containing a program statement. It is considered good programming practice to include comments at the start of a program to explain its purpose. In our case, we have the purpose preceded by the name of the file containing the whole program.

Lines 3 and 4 are called include statements.

```
#include <iostream.h>
#include <string.h>
```

These lines are instructions to the compiler, known as directives. For the moment we shall consider such statements as a means by which the compilation system allows us to use certain of its features. In the first case, the way data is sent to the monitor screen and read from the keyboard; the "io" is an abbreviation for input and output and this statement enables us to use the object **cout** later in the program. In the second case, the way we may use groups of

```
// HELLO.CPP
// A program to display the Hello World message
#include <iostream.h>
#include <string.h>
class message
    {
    public :
        void initialise () ;
        void display () ;
    protected :
        char contents [12] ;
    } ;

void message::initialise ()
    {
    strcpy (contents, "Hello World") ;
    }

void message::display ()
    {
    cout << contents << endl ;
    }

void main ()
    {
    message hello ;
    hello.initialise () ;
    hello.display () ;
    }
```

Figure 3.2

characters called strings; this statement enables us to use the function **strcpy**
later in the program.

The section of code in lines 5 to 12 is a complete object class definition.

```
class message
    {
    public :
        void initialise () ;
        void display () ;
    protected :
        char contents [12] ;
    } ;
```

The object class definition is introduced by the C++ keyword **class** followed by the programmer-chosen class identifier **message**. The whole of the class definition is bounded by braces { and }, and finally terminated by a semicolon. Note that the layout of this section is not a necessary requirement of the C++ language, but indentation has been used to highlight the different component parts.

Within the braces, we declare the functions and data associated with the object class. We have two sections labelled by the C++ keywords **public** and **protected**, note the colon that follows these keywords. We label parts of a class definition in this way to enable or disable the general use of parts of an object class. In general terms, those parts of an object class that are labelled **public** may be used in any part of the program; those labelled **protected** may only be used within the definition of the functions of the object class or its descendants.

In the public part of the class definition, we have two function prototypes called **member function prototypes**. These declare the object class functions. In this case, functions to display and initialise a message. The format consists of three parts: the **result type**, the **identifier** and the **arguments**. We will not concern ourselves with the details of these parts other than in the context of these simple examples. The **result type** here is **void**, meaning that the functions do not produce anything that needs to be classified by type. The programmer-chosen **identifiers** are **display** and **initialise**. The **arguments** of a function are enclosed within parentheses. There are no arguments for these functions, so we simply have the parentheses.

In the protected part of the class definition, we have the declaration of a **member data** item:

```
char contents [12] ;
```

In this statement, we are declaring a text string to contain the contents of the message. The keyword **char** introduces the declaration and defines the type of data to be held, in this case characters. **contents** is the programmer-chosen identifier for that part of memory where the string will be stored. **[12]** is the maximum length of the string in characters. This includes an allowance of one character to hold a special character to mark the end of the string. This is necessary because text strings in C++ may vary in length up to the specified maximum.

In lines 14 to 17 of the program we have the **definition** for the first of two **member functions**.

```
void message::initialise ()
   {
   strcpy (contents, "Hello World") ;
   }
```

The first line of the function is its **heading**. This consists of the same three parts as the associated prototype already described above. However, there are two differences. The programmer-chosen name `initialise` is preceded by the object class identifier `message` followed by the **scope resolution operator** `::`. The technical details for this need not concern us at the moment; briefly, it is needed so that the data defined in the class definition can be accessed within the function. Notice also that there is no semicolon at the end of the function heading, nor at the end after the closing brace.

The details of the function are enclosed within braces, we have just one line that instructs the computer to make a copy of the text `Hello World` and store that copy in the identifier `contents`. This line starts with `strcpy` which is the name of a C++ function that does this. The words `contents` and `"Hello World"` are called the **arguments** of the function `strcpy` and as such are placed in parentheses after the function name. Note that arguments of functions are separated by commas.

Lines 19 to 22 of the program contain the definition of the second function.

```
void message::display ()
    {
    cout << contents << endl ;
    }
```

As with the previous function, the first line is the heading. Again, this corresponds to the associated prototype with the inclusion of `message::`.

Within the braces we have just one line that instructs the computer to direct output to the monitor screen. This line starts with `cout`, the name of an object that has functions to achieve this. The output to be directed to the monitor screen is specified by following `cout` with the operator `<<` and a definition of the output required. In this case we have two output definitions to be handled by `cout`. The first is the identifier `contents`; this indicates to `cout` that the string stored in this identifier is to be displayed on the monitor screen. The second output definition is `endl` (an abbreviation for end of line); this simply indicates to `cout` that the current line must end and the screen cursor is to be placed at the start of the next line.

Line 24 of our program is one that all of our programs will include (or one very similar) to show where program execution begins.

```
void main ()
```

The parentheses indicate to the compiler that `main` is a function with no arguments. The body of the main function is enclosed by braces (lines 25 and 29).

Line 26 is a declaration of the **object `hello`** as an **instance** of the class `message`.

```
message hello ;
```

In effect, it makes a copy of all the members of `message` and gives them the group identifier `hello`. This means that `hello` can be referred to within the function **main** and that all the public parts of its class definition may be used. We see this in the next two statements of the function (in lines 27 and 28).

    hello.initialise () ;

The member function **initialise** for the object **hello** is **called**; this means that the statement(s) within the function definition for **initialise** are executed. Note the format, instance identifier then a full-stop (known as the **dot operator**) then the member function identifier then the parentheses then a semicolon. The result of the function being called will be that **hello**'s copy of **contents** will be given the value **"Hello World"**. To see the way that this is done, please refer again to the description of the function definition for **initialise** of class **message**.

Finally, the **display** member function for the instance **hello** is called.

    hello.display () ;

The result of this will be that the text stored in **contents** (that is, **Hello World**) will be displayed on the monitor screen and the cursor placed at the start of the next line. Again, to see the way that this is done, please refer to the description of the function definition for **display** of class **message**.

Notice that the functions **initialise** and **display** were declared as **public** because they are being used in the function **main**, which is outside the definition of the object class. The string identifier **contents** was declared as **protected** since it is only used within the definition of a member function of the object class **message**.

3.3 Coding style

The layout of the program is of little concern to the compiler. Generally, spaces are not significant. The use of spaces, comments and blank lines is left to the discretion of the programmer. So, it is possible to produce a program that is readily understood by the compiler but is not so easily read by the human reader. You are encouraged to use a layout and style that ensure that your programs are easy to follow and read.

The identifiers created by the programmer are a matter of choice, but give an opportunity to describe the data that is to be contained within them. Again, you are encouraged to always use meaningful identifiers. Normally, an identifier will not exceed 30 characters in length. It must start with either a letter or the underscore character (_) and its remaining characters may be letters, digits or underscore characters.

Notice that the case used to write C++ is significant; for example, **strcpy** is not the same as **STRCPY**. In our first program, we declared an instance of **message** as **hello**, we could not then refer to it in the main program by **Hello**.

Certain items of punctuation are mandatory parts of the C++ language. In our first program you will notice that declarations and statements end with a semicolon. Also note that in lists, such as in the list of arguments of a function, a comma is used to separate components.

C++ contains several keywords such as **void**, each of which has a specific purpose. These keywords must be surrounded by one or more blank characters and they must not be used as identifiers. The full list of C++ keywords is given in appendix C.

3.4 Pseudo-code for a sequence

As mentioned in section 1.7, a sequence using pseudo-code notation consists of a number of statements to be executed presented in the order of execution. Unless the components of a sequence are themselves controlling statements, the statements will be in plain language with no formal syntax. However, we will find that certain phrases tend to be used for like operations.

An example of a sequence using pseudo-code is given in figure 3.3. Here, we show the basic actions of the function **main** from figure 3.2.

```
main
    Declare object hello of type message
    Call hello.initialise
    Call hello.display
```

Figure 3.3

The first line identifies the function name. The next three are a sequence of the actions to be performed in the order given.

A slightly more complex version of the function display could be described in pseudo-code as in figure 3.4.

```
message::display
    Display screen headings
    Display contents of message
    Display screen footings
```

Figure 3.4

Here, the first line identifies the class and the function name. This is followed by a sequence of three actions. Note that they are simply general descriptions of the activities without relying on a formal syntax. The precise details of what to display and where to display the data on the computer screen would obviously need to be specified and implemented in the C++ code. However, the generalisation 'display ...' will suffice at the design stage.

3.5 Exercises

3.5.1   Please refer to the example in figure 3.2, then answer the following questions:
  (a) What is the purpose of lines 1 and 2? If they were removed, what effect would this have on the running of the program?
  (b) Lines 3 and 4 permit the use of what C++ features?
  (c) What do we call the program statements in lines 8 and 9? What do we call the three component parts of each statement (excluding the terminating semicolons)?
  (d) What three things can you say about the data member declaration in line 11?
  (e) What are the differences between the function prototype in line 8 and the corresponding function heading in line 14.
  (f) What does the member function `initialise` do?
  (g) What does the member function `display` do?
  (h) What is the point of line 24 (that is, `void main ()`)?
  (i) What does the declaration in line 26 do?
  (j) The member functions are called in lines 27 and 28. Describe each of the four components of the statements (excluding the terminating semicolon).
  (k) What happens when a function is called?
  (l) Name the five identifiers that are declared and then used in this example? What are the C++ rules for making up identifiers?
  (m) Why are the functions `initialise` and `display` declared as `public`?

3.5.2   Make changes as necessary to the example in figure 3.2 to achieve the following revised specification.

  Allow for two messages to be displayed, the first should be
          `Hello all computer users`
  and the second
          `What a fine day!`
  You should implement this by making the first two lines more appropriate, by replacing the member data declaration in the class definition by two similar statements, and by replacing the single statement in both of the member functions by two similar statements.

3.5.3   Please refer to section 3.4, then answer the following questions:
  (a) What will the first line of the pseudo-code for a function normally contain?
  (b) Give an example of a pseudo-code statement indicating that a function is to be used.
  (c) Rewrite the pseudo-code for the `display` function so that the actions are performed in the reverse order.

4 An Introduction to Inheritance

Objectives for this chapter
Familiarity with the C++ programming terms and concepts:
- the member function `cin.get`
- the data type `char` for a single character
- program files and header files
- use of a prompt for keyboard input
- deriving a new object class from an existing (base) class
- using header files and a derived class
- inheriting object class members.

Ability to:
- understand a simple C++ program that uses a header file
- understand a simple C++ program that uses a derived object class
- write pseudo-code for a simple function
- write simple C++ programs based on the examples in the chapter.

4.1 Using a header file

Our first program in chapter 3 would normally be typed into a single computer file and presented to the compiler for translation and execution to produce the required results. However, we could separate the object class definition and member function definitions from the function **main**. Let us say that we put the defintions in a file called **message.h** and the function **main** in the file called **hello_m.cpp**. The file **message.h** is known as a header file and its contents are shown in figure 4.1. The contents of the program file, **hello_m.cpp**, are shown in figure 4.2.

In figure 4.2 we have the same main function as in figure 3.2 (in chapter 3), preceded by the **#include** statement referencing the header file. When we present the program file to the compiler, as part of the translation process the code from the header file, in effect, replaces the **#include** statement, in the sense that the compiler now regards the program file as being exactly the same as the first program in figure 3.2.

Note that in chapter 3 and figure 4.1 the previous **#include** statements

```
// MESSAGE.H
// The object class message
#include <iostream.h>
#include <string.h>
class message
    {
    public :
        void initialise () ;
        void display () ;
    protected :
        char contents [12] ;
    } ;

void message::initialise ()
    {
    strcpy (contents, "Hello World") ;
    }

void message::display ()
    {
    cout << contents << endl ;
    }
```

Figure 4.1

```
// HELLO_M.CPP
// A program to display the Hello World message
#include "message.h"
void main ()
    {
    message hello ;
    hello.initialise () ;
    hello.display () ;
    }
```

Figure 4.2

reference facilities held in a compiler library and are identified by a name enclosed in angle brackets <>; we now reference the **message.h** file and enclose this name with ", to indicate that it is a file stored in the same directory as the program file.

4.2 Inheriting code from our first program into a second program

The statements in **message.h** can be reused in other programs that require the object class **message** or derivatives based on it. For example, if we wished to have an additional program that accepted any message from the keyboard and then displayed it on the monitor screen, we have a similar model to that described in figure 3.1, but need a different initialisation function. Instead of simply assigning a value of **"Hello World"** to the **contents** of the message, we need code to accept a string of characters into **contents**.

We could simply make a copy of **message.h**, call it a different name and make modifications to the copy. However, there is a better solution to this type of problem that avoids duplicating the code; rather it involves inheriting the code from **message.h** by defining a new object class based on **message**, but with a new member function **initialise**. Hence there is no code duplication, simply a replacement for that part which has different requirements. The model of the new class **any_message** (the derived class) and its derivation from the original class **message** (the base class) is represented by the object schema shown in figure 4.3.

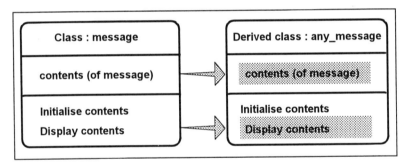

Figure 4.3

As mentioned in chapter 2, notice how the arrows and shading indicate those members of the derived class that have been inherited from the base class without being changed; the lack of shading in the derived class indicates those members that have been added or, in this case, redefined.

We implement this additional program by writing C++ code for a new header file **message1.h** and a new program file **anymess.cpp**. They are shown in figures 4.4 and 4.5 respectively. The pseudo-code for the function **initialise** is also given in figure 4.6.

Let us first describe the contents of the header file line by line.

```
// MESSAGE1.H
// The object class any_message
```

We have described comments before; these identify and reflect the purpose of the new header file.

```
// MESSAGE1.H
// The object class any_message
#include "message.h"
class any_message : public message
    {
    public :
        void initialise () ;
    } ;

void any_message::initialise ()
    {
    char terminator ;
    cout << "Enter message: " ;
    cin.get (contents, 12) ;
    cin.get (terminator) ;
    }
```

Figure 4.4

```
// ANYMESS.CPP
// A program to display any message
#include "message1.h"
void main ()
    {
    any_message do_message ;
    do_message.initialise () ;
    do_message.display () ;
    }
```

Figure 4.5

```
any_message::initialise
    Declare terminator variable
    Prompt for message
    Accept message contents
    Skip newline character
```

Figure 4.6

Line 3 is also familiar.

```
#include "message.h"
```

This statement is a directive to the compiler to take into account (or "include")
all the code found in the file **message.h**.

In lines 4 to 8, we define a new object class based on **message** as previously defined in the file **message.h**.

```
class any_message : public message
   {
   public :
      void initialise () ;
   } ;
```

The first line in this section, introduced by the keyword **class**, specifies the new object class, called **any_message**, derived from the object class **message** with all of its facilities made **public** in the new class. Note the colon after the new class identifier and before the derivation type **public**.

The new object class inherits all of the public and protected components of the class upon which it is based. So we inherit the member data **contents** and two member functions called **initialise** and **display** in our new object class. However, we need to redefine the initialisation function, so we declare a **public** member function **initialise** as part of **any_message**; as before, this is enclosed in braces.

In lines 10 to 16, we have the definition of the new member function **initialise**.

```
void any_message::initialise ()
   {
   char terminator ;
   cout << "Enter message: " ;
   cin.get (contents, 12) ;
   cin.get (terminator) ;
   }
```

After the heading, we have four statements enclosed in braces as usual. The first statement is a data declaration for a single character (indicated by the keyword **char**). The function will refer to this area of data by the identifier **terminator**. The second statement will display text on the monitor screen inviting the user to type a message; this text is called a prompt. We have already described the use of **cout** to display data on the screen, in this case we do not use **endl** because we want to keep the cursor on the same line. The third statement will obtain the message from the keyboard. **cin.get** is a mechanism by which we can obtain, in this case, up to 11 characters from the keyboard and store them in **contents** (with the end of string character being automatically appended). Formally, **get** is a member function of the object **cin** provided by the compiler in **iostream.h**. The first argument of **get** is the identifier of an area to receive the data (**contents**), the second is the maximum length of the data (**12**) including the automatically appended end of string character. It is assumed that after the data has been entered the user presses the enter key. A side-effect of this is that the character generated when the user presses enter (we will call it the newline character) is not transferred to `contents`, and so to avoid it being used by mistake in some later processing, we transfer it to another area called `terminator`. This is achieved by the fourth statement using `cin.get`.

The main program, `anymess.cpp` given in figure 4.5, is very similar to `hello_m.cpp` in figure 4.2. It has the same structure but references a different header file and uses different identifiers. The differences are now described.

In line 3 we have a different include statement.

```
#include "message1.h"
```

The new header file is referenced (instead of `message.h`), but note that `message1.h` does, in turn, reference `message.h`.

The 3 statements of the function `main` refer to the derived class `any_message`.

```
any_message do_message ;
do_message.initialise () ;
do_message.display () ;
```

Here, we have the declaration of an instance of the new object class `any_message` called `do_message`. Then we have the two member function calls. The first invokes the new `initialise` function to prompt for and receive the data. The second calls the inherited `display` function.

It is important to appreciate the relationship between the model in figure 4.3 and the three files that are used in the complete program. The base class `message` is defined in `message.h` (figure 4.1). The file `message1.h` (figure 4.4) uses a `#include` statement to incorporate `message.h` and defines the derived class `any_message`, which inherits the members of `message`, but has a different, overriding, `initialise` function. The program file `anymess.cpp` (figure 4.5) uses a `#include` statement to incorporate `message1.h` and contains the executable code based on an object `do_message` of the class `any_message`.

4.3 Exercises

4.3.1 Please refer to the program in figures 4.1 and 4.2, then answer the following questions:

(a) What is the difference between the two `#include` statements in the header file `message.h` and the one in the program file `hello_m.cpp`?

(b) What is the purpose of the `#include` statement in the program file `hello_m.cpp`?

4.3.2 Please refer to the examples in figures 4.4 and 4.5, then answer the following questions:

(a) Why is line 3 (the **#include** statement) included in the header file **message1.h**?

(b) The first line of the class definition in the header file **message1.h** consists of four words as well as the colon. What is the purpose of each of the four words?

(c) How do you declare a data area for a single character?

(d) The **cout** statement in the header file **message1.h** does not have an **endl**, can you suggest why?

(e) What is the purpose of the first **cin.get** statement? Why does the **cin.get** function have 12 as an argument when **contents** will be of a maximum size of 11?

(f) What is the purpose of the second **cin.get** statement? Why is it necessary?

(g) How does the compiler know which **initialise** member function to use, the one in **message.h** or the one in **message1.h**.

4.3.3 Describe what changes are necessary to the program in figures 4.1 and 4.2 to achieve the following revised specification.

Allow for two messages to be displayed, the first should be

> **Hello all computer users**

and the second

> **What a fine day!**

You should replace the member data statement in the class definition by two similar statements, and replace the statement in each of the member functions by two similar statements.

4.3.4 Describe what changes are necessary to the program in figures 4.4 and 4.5 to achieve the following revised specification.

Allow for two messages to be displayed, the first should be

> **Hello boys**

and the second

> **Hello girls**

You should implement this by amending the program file **anymess.cpp** only.

4.3.5 Produce a new header file **forename.h** (inheriting **message** from **message.h**) and a new program file **assign45.cpp** to achieve the following specification.

Prompt the user of the program to enter their forename, accept the forename from the keyboard, then display it back on the screen. You may assume that the forename will contain at most 11 characters. Before writing the C++ code, produce pseudo-code for the function **initialise**, a member of the class **forename**.

5 Arithmetic

Objectives for this chapter
Familiarity with the C++ programming terms and concepts:
- the data types `int`, `long int` and `float`
- the keyword `const`
- the arithmetic operators `+ - * / % ++ --`
- the precedence of arithmetic operators
- integer and float variable declarations
- assignment statements that use arithmetic expressions
- `cin` and `cout` with `int` and `float` values
- the manipulator `setprecision`.

Ability to:
- develop an object class definition
- use a model and pseudo-code descriptions of the functions of an object class to produce C++ code
- read and understand a simple C++ program that uses integer and real numbers
- write simple C++ programs that use integer and real numbers.

5.1 Integers

In C++ every item of data is considered to be of a specific type. For example, numbers such as 4 and 37 are examples of integers, whereas 6.75 and 2.5 are examples of real numbers. Different data types are stored and manipulated differently within the machine. Consequently, we must define the type of each identifier whenever we declare it in a program.

We can declare the member data for an object class or variables within a function by specifying a type and an identifier (such as `char terminator` in the function `initialise` referred to in the previous chapter). To declare integer member data or variables, we use the type name `int` followed by an appropriate identifier and a semicolon, for example

```
int years_of_age ;
```

A value of type `int` is a whole number lying within limits defined by the compiler. The minimum and maximum integer values for typical C++ systems are `-32768` to `32767`. The values of all integer data items must lie within these limits.

If a larger range is required, then one can use the type `long int` (this can be abbreviated to `long`) which typically has a range of `-2147483648` to `2147483647`. Other integer types are also available.

5.2 Assignment statements and integer arithmetic

In the previous chapter, we used the function `strcpy` to store a string value in the variable identifier `contents` using

```
strcpy (contents, "Hello World") ;
```

For other data types, including integers, a value is copied into a storage location by means of an **assignment statement**. In its simplest form an assignment statement consists of a variable identifier followed by the assignment operator = followed by an expression that will give a value to be placed in the variable. For example,

```
average_age = total_age / no_of_people ;
```

The result of this assignment statement would be that a new value is given to the data item identified by `average_age`. The / symbol is used to denote division. The full range of arithmetic operators used in integer expressions is given in the table in figure 5.1.

Operator	Meaning
++	increase by 1
--	decrease by 1
*	multiply
/	divide
%	give remainder after division
+	add
-	subtract or negate

Figure 5.1

Integer division produces a truncated result (not rounded up or down). For example,

```
average_age = 124 / 5 ;
```

assigns the value 24 to `average_age`.

The **%** operator gives the remainder after division. For example,

```
left_over = 124 % 5 ;
```

assigns the value 4 to **left_over**.

The **++** and **--** operators allow a shorthand for increasing and decreasing by one. For example,

```
++ counter ;
```

increases the value already in **counter** by 1.

When an arithmetic expression involving sub-expressions is evaluated, the normal priorities (precedence) of the above operators apply. Any sub-expression in parentheses is evaluated first, then **++** and **--** have priority over *****, **/** and **%**, which, in turn, have priority over **+** and **-**. When two operators of the same priority are contained within an expression, evaluation is from left to right. The full list of C++ operators in order of precedence is given in appendix C.

Notice that the spaces either side of the operators are optional, but are included to aid readability.

5.3 Real arithmetic

If we want to use real numbers such as 23.75 or 0.5, we use the data type **float**. As with integers we can declare **float** member data in class definitions or variables in functions. For example,

```
float unit_price,
      total_cost ;
```

Each C++ system defines limits on the range (the smallest and largest allowable values) and precision (the maximum number of significant digits) of numbers of type **float**. Any attempt to evaluate a value outside the given range results in overflow (the result is too large) or underflow (the result is too small). For very large or very small real numbers, we use the type **double**.

We use the same basic operators in real expressions that we have already seen in integer expressions except for the **%** operator that obviously has an application only with integers.

C++ allows you to mix integers and real numbers in arithmetic expressions. As each part of the expression is evaluated, if both operands are integers, the resulting value will be of type **int**; but if either or both of the operands are real numbers, the resulting value will be of type **float**.

5.4 A model for a student's assessment in a subject

A program is required to process a single student's examination mark and practical mark for a single module. The module identity, student identity, examination mark and practical mark will be obtained from the keyboard, then the sum of the marks and the weighted average of the marks will be displayed after first displaying the identities and the marks. The weighted average is given by (examination mark) x 0.75 + (practical mark) x 0.25.

A typical dialogue for this program is shown in figure 5.2. The first four lines demonstrate the acquisition of the input values. The lines that follow are output as a result of processing the input.

```
Enter module identity code GEOG
Enter student identity code MK321
Enter examination mark 67
Enter practical mark 56

Student identity: MK321 for Module: GEOG
Exam mark is 67 Practical mark is 56
The sum of the marks is 123

Student identity: MK321 for Module: GEOG
Exam mark is 67 Practical mark is 56
The weighted average of the marks is 64.3
```

Figure 5.2

We will use an approach similar to that outlined in the previous chapter to develop the program.

The object class to achieve this will need six data items: a module identity code, a student identity code, an examination mark, a practical mark, the weighted average of the two marks, and the sum of the two marks. A function will be needed to initialise the object by accepting both the identity codes (as strings) and both the marks (as integers) from the keyboard, and then calculating the sum of the marks and the weighted average. Other functions will display the module and student identities, the marks, the sum of the marks, and the weighted average of the marks.

The model for the object class is given in figure 5.3 and pseudo-code representations of the functions are given in figure 5.4.

Notice that since we have to display the module and student identities and the marks when displaying the sum of the marks and when displaying the weighted average, we have described the functions **display_identities** and **display_marks** and then called them from both **display_sum** and **display_weighted_average**.

Figure 5.5 shows that part of the header file **marks.h** that contains the object class definition.

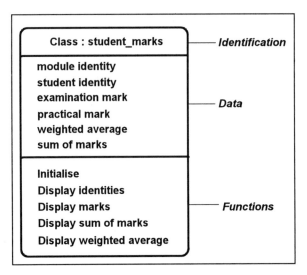

Figure 5.3

```
student_marks::initialise
   Declare terminator variable
   Prompt for and accept module identity
   Prompt for and accept student identity
   Prompt for and accept examination mark
   Prompt for and accept practical mark
   Calculate the sum of the marks
   Calculate the weighted average

student_marks::display_identities
   Display the module and student identities

student_marks::display_marks
   Display the two marks

student_marks::display_sum
   Call display_identities
   Call display_marks
   Display the sum of the marks

student_marks::display_weighted_average
   Call display_identities
   Call display_marks
   Display the weighted average
```

Figure 5.4

```
// MARKS.H
// The object class student_marks
#include <iostream.h>
#include <iomanip.h>
class student_marks
   {
   public :
      void initialise () ;
      void display_identities () ;
      void display_marks () ;
      void display_sum () ;
      void display_weighted_average () ;
   protected :
      char   student_identity [9] ;
      char   module_identity [6] ;
      int    exam_mark,
             practical_mark,
             sum ;
      float weighted_average ;
   } ;
```

Figure 5.5

You will notice several statements that are similar to those found in our previous examples. First notice a new **#include** statement.

```
#include <iomanip.h>
```

This statement references a compiler header file that contains manipulators for formatting output. The need for this will become apparent when we look at the output of a real number.

After the keyword **protected,** we have the declaration of six data members.

```
char   student_identity [9] ;
char   module_identity [6] ;
int    exam_mark,
       practical_mark,
       sum ;
float weighted_average ;
```

The first two, strings, are similar to those used in the previous programs. The next is a declaration of three integers. In this example, the declaration is in the form of a list with the type **int** preceding a list of three identifiers separated by commas. It is not necessary to present identifiers of the same type in a list, we could write them as separate declarations:

```
int   practical_mark ;
```

```
int   exam_mark ;
int   sum ;
```

The final declaration is for a real number. Declarations of real numbers follow the same pattern as integers in that either a single programmer-chosen identifier or a list of identifiers separated by commas follow the keyword for the type **float**.

5.5 Using integer and real numbers, the `initialise` function

Figure 5.6 contains the **initialise** function from the header file **marks.h**. It uses both integer and real arithmetic.

```
void student_marks::initialise ()
   {
   const float exam_weight = 0.75,
               practical_weight = 0.25 ;
   char terminator ;
   cout << "Enter module identity code " ;
   cin.get (module_identity, 6) ;
   cin.get (terminator) ;
   cout << "Enter student identity code " ;
   cin.get (student_identity, 9) ;
   cout << "Enter examination mark " ;
   cin >> exam_mark ;
   cout << "Enter practical mark " ;
   cin >> practical_mark ;
   cin.get (terminator) ;
   sum = exam_mark + practical_mark ;
   weighted_average = exam_mark * exam_weight +
      practical_mark * practical_weight ;
   }
```

Figure 5.6

There are a number of new concepts introduced in this example, so we will describe these line by line.

After the function heading and opening brace, we have the following in lines 3 and 4.

```
const float exam_weight = 0.75,
            practical_weight = 0.25 ;
```

Recall that in the object class definition we had a data member described by:

```
float weighted_average ;
```

Now we have a declaration that is a list of two **float** constants. They are similar to variable declarations in the sense that storage is allocated for them and they must be of a particular data type, but because they are introduced with the keyword **const** they must be given a value that will not change. The values to be permanently associated with the identifiers are placed after the identifiers and are introduced by the = sign.

Using constant identifiers can make the program easier to maintain. Suppose that these weightings are used in numerous assignment statements throughout the function and at some time in the future their values have to be changed. If the actual values have been used in the assignment statements, then each statement will have to be changed. If constant identifiers are used, then we only need to change the values in the **const** declaration.

The next six lines of the **initialise** member function are similar to those in the example program in the previous chapter.

```
char terminator ;
cout << "Enter module identity code " ;
cin.get (module_identity, 6) ;
cin.get (terminator) ;
cout << "Enter student identity code " ;
cin.get (student_identity, 9) ;
```

We declare the **char** variable **terminator**, then use **cout** to display a prompt, then use **cin.get** to obtain up to 5 characters from the keyboard for the module identity, terminated when the user presses the enter key. We use **cin.get** to skip over the character (newline) generated by using the enter key, then use **cout** and **cin.get** to obtain the student identity. Note that in this latter case, we do not need to follow the **cin.get** with another one to skip over the newline character. This is because, as explained below, the next **cin** statement ignores any such characters in the input stream.

The acquisition of the examination and practical marks follows a similar pattern.

```
cout << "Enter examination mark " ;
cin >> exam_mark ;
cout << "Enter practical mark " ;
cin >> practical_mark ;
cin.get (terminator) ;
```

For each of the two integer marks, we have a prompt using **cout** followed by **cin**. This use of **cin** does not need to reference the member function **get**, it is simply followed by the operator **>>** and the identifier for the appropriate data item.

Note that when we accepted a string from the keyboard using **cin.get**, we assumed that the end of the string would be signified by the newline character. In this example, we make the same assumption for the integers. However, there is a difference in the processing as we have already intimated. When **cin** is used to obtain numeric data it will first ignore **white-space** characters (that is, a blank, a tab, a newline or a carriage return) before transferring the data value to the nominated area. So, we do not need to precede `cin` by a statement to skip over a newline character, but it is good practice to ensure that the final newline character is processed to avoid it being used by mistake in some later processing.

The C++ code to calculate the sum of the two marks is a straightforward example of using integer arithmetic.

```
sum = exam_mark + practical_mark ;
```

Here we have a single assignment statement that places the sum of the contents of `exam_mark` and `practical_mark` into `sum`. The original contents of `sum` are irrelevant to the calculation and are lost after the assignment has been made.

In the last two lines of the `initialise` function we have the calculation of the weighted average. This is an example of real arithmetic.

```
weighted_average = exam_mark * exam_weight +
    practical_mark * practical_weight ;
```

The calculation of the weighted average is achieved in a single assignment statement. Note that because of the precedence rules for the arithmetic operators, the two multiplication operations are done first followed by the addition of the results of the multiplication operations. Note also, that we are using the constants declared at the beginning of the function. If we did not have these constants, we would have written the assignment statement as:

```
weighted_average = exam_mark * 0.75 +
    practical_mark * 0.25 ;
```

5.6 The display functions

Figures 5.7, 5.8, 5.9 and 5.10 contain the `display_identities`, `display_marks`, `display_sum` and `display_weighted_average` functions from the header file `marks.h`.

```
void student_marks::display_identities ()
   {
   cout << endl ;
   cout << "Student identity: " << student_identity
      << " for Module: " << module_identity
      << endl ;
   }
```

Figure 5.7

```
void student_marks::display_marks ()
   {
   cout << "Exam mark is " << exam_mark <<
      " Practical mark is " << practical_mark
      << endl ;
   }
```

Figure 5.8

```
void student_marks::display_sum ()
   {
   display_identities () ;
   display_marks () ;
   cout << "The sum of the marks is " << sum <<
      endl ;
   }
```

Figure 5.9

```
void student_marks::display_weighted_average ()
   {
   display_identities () ;
   display_marks () ;
   cout << "The weighted average of the marks is "
      << setprecision (1) << weighted_average <<
      endl ;
   }
```

Figure 5.10

The `display_sum` function uses by now familiar code. After calling the two functions `display_identities` and `display_marks`, we use `cout` to display a message followed by the contents of `sum`.

If we had not calculated the sum in the `initialise` function, we could have incorporated the calculation directly within the `cout` statement by:

```
cout << "The sum of the marks is " << exam_mark +
   practical_mark << endl ;
```

Likewise, after the heading for the `display_weighted_average` function and the calls to `display_identities` and `display_marks`, we have a `cout` statement to output the results.

```
cout << "The weighted average of the marks is "
   << setprecision (1) << weighted_average <<
   endl ;
```

The statement to produce the output uses **cout** as usual, but this time it has an extra component, **setprecision (1)**. This is known as a **manipulator** because it manipulates the way in which the floating point output is to be produced, in this case with one digit after the decimal point. Manipulators are defined in the compiler header file **iomanip.h**. They are necessary because the default or standard way for **cout** to produce output is simply to take as much space as it needs for the given values. For floating point output we may not want many places of decimals, so we define the precision and get a rounded result when necessary.

Finally, figure 5.11 is included to show a typical program file (**subject.cpp**) that creates the object and invokes the member functions to produce the dialogue given in figure 5.2.

```
// SUBJECT.CPP
// A program to produce the weighted average of a
// student's assessment marks for a subject
#include "marks.h"
void main ()
    {
    student_marks geography_MK321 ;
    geography_MK321.initialise () ;
    geography_MK321.display_sum () ;
    geography_MK321.display_weighted_average () ;
    }
```

Figure 5.11

5.7 Exercises

5.7.1 Please refer to the example in figure 5.5, then answer the following questions:

(a) In what other way could the lines declaring the integer variables have been written?

(b) What keyword introduces the declaration of a real number?

(c) What is the purpose of the second **#include** statement?

(d) How many characters are allowed for in the student identity?

5.7.2 Please refer to the example in figure 5.6, then answer the following questions:

(a) In the member function **initialise**, why do we not immediately follow the third **cin.get** statement (for **student_identity**) with another one to skip over the newline character?

(b) What is the assignment operator in C++?

(c) What purpose does the keyword **const** serve in the data declaration in **initialise**?

(d) With reference to the assignment statement that calculates the weighted average, if **exam_mark** had the value 40 and **practical_mark** had the value 50, would the weighted average be computed as 42.5 or 20.0? Explain why you have chosen the answer you have and why the alternative given is incorrect.

5.7.3   Please refer to the functions in figures 5.7 to 5.10, then answer the following questions:

(a) If **sum** was not a data member, explain why the statement to calculate the sum in the function **initialise** should be removed.

(b) Given that **student_identity** has the value **EG100**, **module_identity** has the value **HIST**, **exam_mark** has the value **60** and **practical_mark** has the value **66**, what would be displayed on the monitor screen by the function **display_sum**? Where does the screen cursor end up?

(c) What does the manipulator **setprecision (1)** do in **display_weighted_average**?

5.7.4   Make changes as necessary to the example in figures 5.6 to achieve the following revised specification.

The weighted average is computed by adding one fifth of the value of the practical mark to four fifths of the value of the examination mark.

5.7.5   Produce a new header file **marks55.h** (inheriting **student_marks** from **marks.h** to derive a new class **student_marks_55**) and a new program file **assign55.cpp** to achieve the following specification.

Use the function **initialise** inherited from **student_marks** to prompt the user of the program to enter the identities and the two marks (as before). Then call a function to compute the average (a **float** data member) of the examination mark and the practical mark (by dividing the sum by 2.0) without displaying the result. Then call a separate function to display the two marks followed on a separate line by the computed average; this function should use an inherited function to display the two marks.

5.7.6   Produce a header file (**circle.h**) and a program file (**assign56.cpp**) to produce a dialogue on the monitor screen as demonstrated in figure 5.12. The specification is described by the model in figure 5.13 and the pseudo-code in figure 5.14 for the member functions and figure 5.15 for the main program.

```
Enter radius of circle in centimetres 10
The area of the circle is 314.16 square cms
The circumference of the circle is 62.83 cms
```

Figure 5.12

```
Class : circle

radius (float)
pi (float)

Initialise pi and radius
Display area
Display circumference
```

Figure 5.13

```
circle::initialise
    Declare terminator variable
    Initialise pi = 3.1416
    Prompt for and accept radius

circle::display_area
    Declare area variable
    Calculate area (πr²)
    Display area

circle::display_circumference
    Declare circumference variable
    Calculate circumference (2πr)
    Display circumference
```

Figure 5.14

```
main
    Declare disk of type circle
    Call disk.initialise
    Call disk.display_area
    Call disk.display_circumference
```

Figure 5.15

6 An Introduction to Selection

Objectives for this chapter
Familiarity with C++ programming terms and concepts:
- the keywords `if`, `if-else`
- relational expressions
- relational operators
- compound conditions
- nested selections.

Ability to:
- understand a simple C++ program that uses `if`, and `if-else`
- write simple C++ programs that use `if`, and `if-else`
- write pseudo-code using selection constructs.

6.1 Further development of a model for a student's assessment in a subject

As mentioned in section 1.7, a selection involves choosing between two or more different actions depending on the value of a data item or some condition. We can illustrate the concept of selecting different actions and the associated C++ language constructs by developing further the student marks example from chapter 5. This will involve taking different actions depending on the values of the examination mark and the practical mark.

We can use inheritance to derive a new class from **student_marks** in **marks.h**, called **student_marks_1**, with additional member functions. The object schema in figure 6.1 shows how the revised model is derived. Figure 6.2 contains the new object class definition from **marks1.h**.

6.2 The `if` statement

As with most languages, C++ has a construct, namely the `if` statement, enabling the programmer to choose between different actions according to the value of a condition. The condition is an expression that gives a value of true or false.

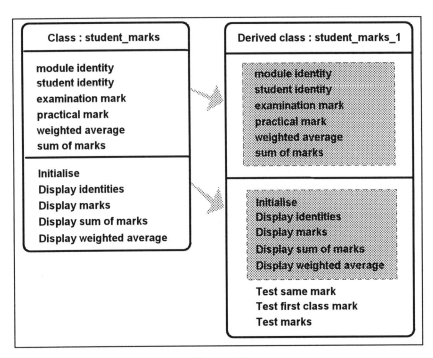

Figure 6.1

```
// MARKS1.H
// The object class student_marks_1
#include "marks.h"
class student_marks_1 : public student_marks
   {
   public :
      void test_same_mark () ;
      void test_first_class_mark () ;
      void test_marks () ;
   } ;
```

Figure 6.2

We will use a simple form of the **if** statement in the new member function, **test_same_mark**, to display an appropriate message if the practical mark and the examination mark have the same value. The pseudo-code for this function is shown in figure 6.3.

In the selection, we have a single statement to be executed when the condition specified in the **IF** is found to be true. The operation that is governed by the condition is indented beneath the **IF** statement. Although not demonstrated in this example, it is possible to have more than one operation that is

```
student_marks_1::test_same_mark
   Call display_identities
   Call display_marks
   IF the marks are the same
       Display same marks message
   Display a blank line
```

Figure 6.3

executed when a condition is true, in which case they would be written at the same indentation, as we shall see in section 6.6.

The C++ code from **marks1.h** for the function **test_same_mark** is given in figure 6.4.

```
void student_marks_1::test_same_mark ()
   {
   display_identities () ;
   display_marks () ;
   if (exam_mark == practical_mark)
       cout << "The marks are the same" << endl ;
   cout << endl ;
   }
```

Figure 6.4

Notice particularly the **if** statement in **test_same_mark**.

```
if (exam_mark == practical_mark)
    cout << "The marks are the same" << endl ;
```

This statement will display the **cout** message only if the contents of **exam_mark** and **practical_mark** have the same value. The statement is introduced by the keyword **if**, then a **condition** (or **relational expression**) in parentheses followed by the statement to be executed when the condition is true. The condition, in this example, uses the **relational operator** **==** which means test the value of the operand (an expression or, in this case the single variable) that appears to its left for equality with the value of the operand (expression or, single variable) that appears to its right.

The comparison must give an answer of true (they are equal) or false (they are not equal). If an answer of true is given, then the statement associated with the **if** (the **cout** statement to display the message in this example) is executed followed by the next statement after the **if** (that is, the **cout** statement to give a blank line). If an answer of false is given, the **cout** statement to display a message would be ignored and the **cout** statement to give a blank line would be executed directly. We can see the sequence of operations in the operation flow diagram at figure 6.5.

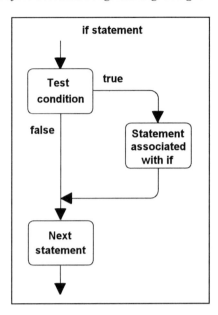

Figure 6.5

6.3 The if-else statement

A slightly different form of the **if** statement allows us to define actions for both true and false results of the condition. This is demonstrated in the function **test_first_class_mark**, where we display two different messages depending on whether or not the examination mark is at least 70. The pseudo-code for this function is given in figure 6.6.

Here, we have a single statement (**Display first class exam mark message**) to be executed when the condition specified in the IF is found to be true and a single statement (**Display not first class exam mark message**) to be executed if the condition is not true. The operations that are governed by both the condition and its alternative are indented underneath the **IF** and **ELSE** respectively. Again, there could have been a number of statements associated with the **IF** or the **ELSE**.

Considering the C++ code in figure 6.7, we note that in the **if** statement, as in the first example, the comparison of the two operands must give an answer of true (**exam_mark** is greater than or equal to 70) or false (**exam_mark** is less than 70). If the answer is true, then the statement associated with the **if**, the first **cout** statement, is executed. If the answer is false, the statement associated with the keyword **else**, the second **cout** statement, is executed. In either case the next statement, the **cout** statement to give a blank line, is always executed.

```
student_marks_1::test_first_class_mark
   Call display_identities
   Call display_marks
   IF exam mark is at least 70
      Display first class exam mark message
   ELSE
      Display not first class exam mark message
   Display a blank line
```

Figure 6.6

```
void student_marks_1::test_first_class_mark ()
   {
   display_identities () ;
   display_marks () ;
   if (exam_mark >= 70)
      cout << "First class exam mark" << endl ;
   else
      cout << "Not a first class exam mark" << endl ;
   cout << endl ;
   }
```

Figure 6.7

Note the necessary semicolons that follow both the statement that is associated with the **if** and the statement that is associated with the **else** (the statements that display messages). The indentation style adopted is not a C++ rule, but is used to enhance the readability of the code.

The sequence of operations for the **if-else** statement is shown in the operation flow diagram at figure 6.8.

6.4 Relational operators

A condition is evaluated as true or false when the value of an expression is compared with the value of another expression in a number of ways. The type of comparison depends on the **relational operator** that is used. The relational operators that we use in C++ are shown in the table given in figure 6.9.

Four of the relational operators have two characters. These are always written as consecutive characters; there must not be any spaces between them.

The operands in **if** statements may be complete expressions, so it is necessary to establish an order of precedence for the relational operators and other C++ operators such as the arithmetic operators. Relational operators have lower priority than arithmetic operators. This means that arithmetic is done first before a comparison is made in conditions such as the following.

```
(2 * exam_mark == practical_mark + 30)
```

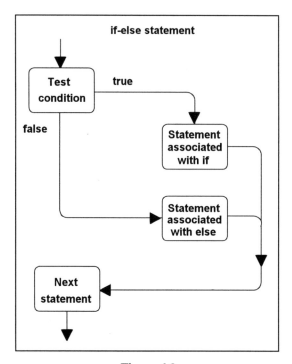

Figure 6.8

Operator	Type of comparison
==	equality
!=	inequality (or not equal)
<	first operand less than second
<=	first operand less than or equal to the second
>	first operand greater than second
>=	first operand greater than or equal to the second

Figure 6.9

6.5 Nested selections

The statement associated with an **if** or an **else** may itself be a conditional (**if**) statement. This means that we can write programs with many related conditional statements.

In the function **test_marks**, we compare the examination mark with the practical mark and display an appropriate message. The pseudo-code for this function is shown in figure 6.10 and the C++ code from **marks1.h** is shown in figure 6.11.

```
student_marks_1::test_marks
   Call display_identities
   Call display_marks
   IF the marks are the same
      Display same marks message
   ELSE IF exam mark is higher than practical mark
      Display exam mark better message
   ELSE
      Display practical mark better message
   Display a blank line
```

Figure 6.10

```
void student_marks_1::test_marks ()
   {
   display_identities () ;
   display_marks () ;
   if (exam_mark == practical_mark)
      cout << "The marks are the same" << endl ;
   else if (exam_mark > practical_mark)
      cout << "Exam mark is better" << endl ;
   else
      cout << "Practical mark is better" << endl ;
   cout << endl ;
   }
```

Figure 6.11

Let us consider the **if-else** statements in the function **test_marks**. We can now see that three different messages may be displayed representing the three possibilities that could arise when comparing the two marks: they could be the same, or the examination mark could be higher or the practical mark could be higher.

For the first **if** statement, we have a **cout** statement to display **"The marks are the same"** (to be executed if the condition is true) associated with the **if**. The statement associated with the corresponding **else** (to be executed if the condition is false) is another **if-else** statement with its own condition and its own statements for **if** (true) and **else** (false). We say that the second **if-else** is nested within the **else** part of the first. This concept and the relationship of the statements is depicted in the operation flow diagram in figure 6.12.

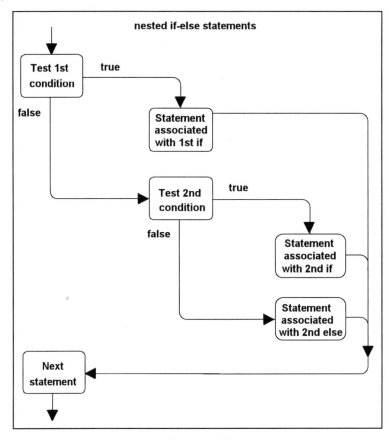

Figure 6.12

Notice that only one of the three messages will be displayed and that there is no need to include the condition

```
if (practical_mark > exam_mark)
```

with the second **else**. If we reach this **else** then we know from the first two conditions that the marks are <u>not</u> equal and the exam mark is <u>not</u> greater than the practical mark. It follows that, at this point, the practical mark must be the higher of the two.

6.6 Compound statements

We have so far assumed that the alternative actions are single statements. If we want these actions to consist of a number of statements, then we use braces { ... } to make a sequence of statements into a single **compound statement**. As we shall see later, compound statements will occur quite frequently in a number of contexts.

Consider the revised version of **test_marks** given first in pseudo-code in figure 6.13.

```
student_marks_1::test_marks
   Call display_identities
   IF the marks are the same
      Display same marks message
      Display (same) mark
   ELSE IF exam mark is higher than practical mark
      Display exam mark better message
      Display exam mark then practical mark
   ELSE
      Display practical mark better message
      Display practical mark then exam mark
   Display a blank line
```

Figure 6.13

Notice that in the pseudo-code, no braces are used; indentation is used to convey the correct meaning.

The C++ code for the revised test_marks is given in figure 6.14. In this example, we have more than one **cout** statement, with braces around them, for each path. Notice where we do and do not have semicolons, in particular, there is no semicolon after any of the right braces (**}**). Also, notice that for compound statements, we have used the indentation convention that we introduced earlier for single statements.

Braces may also be used with a single statement, this is sometimes useful in nested **if** statements to make the code more readable.

Finally, a sample program file (**physics.cpp**) that uses the header file (**marks1.h**) is given in figure 6.15.

6.7 Exercises

6.7.1 Please refer to the example in figure 6.3, then answer the following questions:
(a) What two basic programming constructs are used in the pseudo-code?
(b) When will the same marks message not be produced?
(c) What would the sequence of operations be when both the exam mark and the practical mark have a value of 50?
(d) How do we distinguish the operations that are performed when a condition in an IF is true?

```
void student_marks_1::test_marks ()
   {
   display_identities () ;
   if (exam_mark == practical_mark)
      {
      cout << "The marks are the same" ;
      cout << "  both are " << exam_mark << endl ;
      }
   else if (exam_mark > practical_mark)
      {
      cout << "The exam mark is better" << endl ;
      cout << "The exam mark is " << exam_mark ;
      cout << " the practical mark is " <<
         practical_mark << endl ;
      }
   else
      {
      cout << "The practical mark is better" <<
         endl ;
      cout << "The practical mark is " <<
         practical_mark ;
      cout << " the exam mark is " << exam_mark <<
         endl ;
      }
   cout << endl ;
   }
```

Figure 6.14

```
// PHYSICS.CPP
// A program to test a student's marks
#include "marks1.h"
void main ()
   {
   student_marks_1 physics_MK110 ;
   physics_MK110.initialise () ;
   physics_MK110.test_same_mark () ;
   physics_MK110.test_first_class_mark () ;
   physics_MK110.test_marks () ;
}
```

Figure 6.15

6.7.2 Please refer to the example in figure 6.4, then answer the following questions:
  (a) What are the possible outcomes when a conditional expression is evaluated?
  (b) What are the three basic components of lines 5 and 6?
  (c) Under what circumstances would the execution of line 5 be immediately followed by execution of the statement in line 7?

6.7.3 Please refer to the example in figure 6.7, then answer the following questions:
  (a) What are the five basic components of lines 5 to 8?
  (b) Write two **if** statements (with no **else**) that give the equivalent result to that obtained in lines 5 to 8? Is this code better or worse than that given in the example? Give your reasoning.
  (c) What is the 'greater than or equal to' operator in C++?

6.7.4 Please refer to the example in figure 6.11, then answer the following questions:
  (a) In what sense do we say that we have a nested selection here?
  (b) Write three **if** statements (with no **else**) that give the equivalent result to that obtained in lines 5 to 10? Is this code better or worse than that given in the example? Give your reasoning.
  (c) What is the rule for when to use a semicolon and when not to in a nested selection?
  (d) The style of indentation of the nested **if** statements does not highlight the nesting in the same way as the diagram in figure 6.12. Rewrite the code so as to use a different style of indentation that relates more closely to the diagram?

6.7.5 Please refer to the example in figure 6.14, then answer the following questions:
  (a) What is a compound statement?
  (b) What is the rule for when to use a semicolon and when not to in a nested selection when we have compound statements?
  (c) Rewrite the function **test_marks** without using compound statements for any of the alternative actions in the **if-else** statements. Hint: you will first need to define three new functions.

6.7.6 Rewrite the pseudo-code in figure 6.13 so that a blank line followed by both marks followed by another blank line are displayed if the exam mark and practical mark are both over 65; the exam mark followed by a blank line are displayed if just the exam mark is over 65; the practical mark followed by a blank line are displayed if just the practical mark is over 65.

6.7.7 Rewrite the nested **if-else** statements in figure 6.14 as a single **if-else** statement that displays either

```
The exam mark is worse
The marks are not the same
```

or
```
The practical mark is worse
The marks are not the same
```

6.7.8   Produce a header file (**rectang.h**) and a program file
(**assign68.cpp**) to achieve the following specification.

A program is required to calculate the area and perimeter of a rectangle
and display the results with two decimal places. The user enters the
length and width; a value of zero for the width indicates that the
rectangle is a square. The dialogue on the screen will have the form
given in figure 6.16 or figure 6.17.

```
Enter length of rectangle in centimetres 16.81
Enter width of rectangle in centimetres 9.24
The area is 165.32 square centimetres
The perimeter is 52.10 centimetres
```

Figure 6.16

```
Enter length of rectangle in centimetres 11.46
Enter width of rectangle in centimetres 0
Rectangle is a square
The area is 131.33 square centimetres
The perimeter is 45.84 centimetres
```

Figure 6.17

The model is shown as an object schema in figure 6.18. The pseudo-
code is in figure 6.19 for the member functions and figure 6.20 for the
main program.

```
┌─────────────────────────────────────┐
│  ┌────────────────────────────────┐ │
│  │      Class : rectangle         │ │
│  ├────────────────────────────────┤ │
│  │  length (float)                │ │
│  │  width (float)                 │ │
│  ├────────────────────────────────┤ │
│  │  Initialise width and length   │ │
│  │  Display area                  │ │
│  │  Display perimeter             │ │
│  └────────────────────────────────┘ │
└─────────────────────────────────────┘
```

Figure 6.18

```
rectangle::initialise
   Declare terminator variable
   Prompt for and accept length
   Prompt for and accept width (maybe zero)

rectangle::display_area
   Declare area variable
   IF width is zero (rectangle is a square)
      Display rectangle is a square message
      Calculate area (length * length)
   ELSE
      Calculate area (length * width)
   Display area

rectangle::display_perimeter
   Declare perimeter variable
   IF rectangle is a square
      Calculate perimeter (4 * length)
   ELSE
      Calculate perimeter (2 * length + 2 * length)
   Display perimeter
```

Figure 6.19

```
main
   Declare mouse_mat of type rectangle
   Call mouse_mat.initialise
   Call mouse_mat.display_area
   Call mouse_mat.display_perimeter
```

Figure 6.20

7 Further Concepts for Selection

Objectives for this chapter

Familiarity with C++ programming terms and concepts:
- logical operators **!** (not), **&&** (and) and **||** (or)
- assigning and comparing data of type **char**
- the keyword **switch**
- the use of a type cast.

Ability to:
- understand a simple C++ program that uses logical operators and **switch**
- write simple C++ programs that use logical operators and **switch**.

7.1 Further development of a model for a student's assessment in a subject

We can further illustrate the concept of selecting different actions and the associated C++ language constructs by using a different development to the student marks example from chapter 5. Again this will involve taking different actions depending on the values of the examination mark and the practical mark.

As in the previous chapter, we can use inheritance to derive a new class from **student_marks** in **marks.h**, this time called **student_marks_2**. The derived class will have two new member functions and a redefinition of the function **initialise** as well as a new data member to hold a grade letter. The object schema in figure 7.1 shows how the revised model is derived and figure 7.2 contains the new object class definition from **marks2.h**.

7.2 Logical operators

Conditional (or relational) expressions involving more than a single comparison can be constructed using logical operators (and, or) to connect two or more relational expressions. In addition a relational expression can be negated by the use of another logical operator (not). The logical operators available in C++ are shown in the table given in figure 7.3.

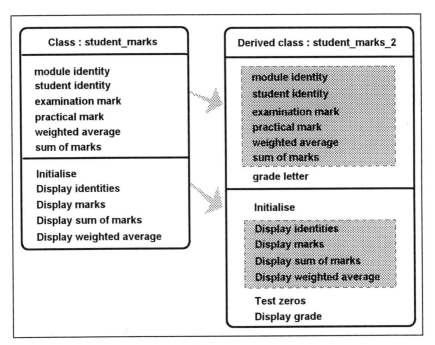

Figure 7.1

```
// MARKS2.H
// The object class student_marks_2
#include "marks.h"
class student_marks_2 : public student_marks
   {
   public :
      void initialise () ;
      void test_zeros () ;
      void display_grade () ;
   protected :
      char grade_letter ;
   } ;
```

Figure 7.2

Operator	Meaning
!	not (negation)
&&	and
||	or

Figure 7.3

The function **test_zeros** illustrates the use of logical operators. The pseudo-code for this function is given in figure 7.4 and the C++ code is in figure 7.5.

```
student_marks_2::test_zeros
   IF both the marks are zero
      Call display_identities
      Display both marks zero message
      Display a blank line
   IF either mark is zero
      Call display_identities
      Display at least one mark zero message
      IF the exam mark is not zero
         Display exam mark not zero message
      IF the practical mark is not zero
         Display practical mark not zero message
      Display a blank line
```

Figure 7.4

```
void student_marks_2::test_zeros ()
   {
   if ((exam_mark == 0) && (practical_mark == 0))
      {
      display_identities () ;
      cout << "Both marks are zero" << endl ;
      cout << endl ;
      }
   if ((exam_mark == 0) || (practical_mark == 0))
      {
      display_identities () ;
      cout << "At least one mark is zero" << endl ;
      if (exam_mark != 0)
         cout << "The exam mark is not zero" <<
            endl ;
      if (! (practical_mark == 0))
         cout << "The practical mark is not zero"
            << endl ;
      cout << endl ;
      }
   }
```

Figure 7.5

Let us examine the first `if` statement in this example.

```
if ((exam_mark == 0) && (practical_mark == 0))
```

In this statement, we have two conditional expressions joined by the logical operator `&&` (and). This means that both of the simple expressions must be true for the whole compound expression to be true. The compound statement associated with the `if` will only be executed if the examination mark is equal to zero and the practical mark is equal to zero. If either of these two expressions is false then the compound statement will not be executed.

Notice that each of the two simple conditional expressions is enclosed in parentheses. This is not a requirement of the language because relational operators have higher priority than logical operators, but it does help to make the whole statement more clear. The whole of the compound conditional expression, however, is enclosed by parentheses as a necessary part of the C++ language.

In the second `if` statement, we have two simple expressions joined by the logical operator `||` (or).

```
if ((exam_mark == 0) || (practical_mark == 0))
```

In this case, only one of the simple expressions needs to be true for the whole of the compound conditional expression to be true. Therefore, if the examination mark is zero the compound statement that follows will be executed irrespective of the value of the practical mark. Similarly, if the practical mark is zero, the compound statement will be executed irrespective of whether the examination mark is zero or not. If both the marks happen to be zero, then again the compound statement associated with the `if` will be executed.

The third `if` statement introduces the inequality operator.

```
if (exam_mark != 0)
    cout << "The exam mark is not zero" << endl ;
```

One way of testing that a value is not zero is to use the `!=` (not equals) operator as in the above. An alternative way of expressing this condition is given in the fourth `if` statement.

```
if (! (practical_mark == 0))
    cout << "The practical mark is not zero"
        << endl ;
```

Here we use the `!` (not) operator. The effect of this operator is to negate the condition following it, that is, it changes false to true or true to false. In this case, the `cout` statement will only be executed if 'practical mark equals zero' is false.

From this example, we might conclude that using the `!=` (not equals) operator is easier. However, there are occasions when it is preferable to use the `!` (not) operator. Suppose, for example, we wanted to change the test in the first `if` to give the message "At least one mark is NOT zero", we would then use:

```
if (! ((exam_mark == 0) && (practical_mark == 0)))
   cout << "At least one mark is NOT zero" << endl ;
```

As with arithmetic operators, there are rules governing the order in which logical operators are applied. The order of priority is **!** (not), then **&&** (and), then **| |** (or). To negate the whole of the compound expression in the above code, we have to put it in parentheses to override the precedence of the **!** operator.

7.3 Assigning and comparing characters

The object class **student_marks_2** contains a new data item that will contain a single letter (A, B, C, D or E) representing the grade obtained by the student for a particular module. It is declared in **marks2.h**, figure 7.2, as:

```
char grade_letter ;
```

A value of type **char** is restricted to what can be contained in one byte. For example, we have already used

```
char terminator ;
```

and stored the newline character in this variable.

Variables and constants of type **char** are usually used when processing single characters such as a letter of the alphabet, a single digit or a punctuation character. Within a C++ program, a value of type **char** is normally denoted by a single character enclosed in apostrophes, for example

```
'D'     '2'     'r'     '?'
```

As with **int** and **float**, character values and variables can be used in assignment statements, for example

```
grade_letter = 'B' ;
```

Most computers use the ASCII character codes. ASCII is the acronym given to an international standard concerned with data communication. It associates a unique numeric value for each character. For example, the digits '0' though to '9' have values 48 to 57, the upper case letters 'A' through to 'Z' have values 65 to 90 and the lower case letters 'a' through to 'z' have values 97 to 122. (See Appendix D for the complete set of characters and corresponding values.) This means that characters can be easily compared using the standard relational operators; the ordering is given by the corresponding ASCII code. For example, the following expressions would all yield true:

```
('F' < 'M')     ('9' >= '2')     ('a' != 'A')
```

The logical operator **&&**, introduced in the previous section, can be used to determine whether or not a variable holds a value within a specific range. To test whether or not the character held in **char_value** was a digit, we would use:

```
if ((char_value >= '0') && (char_value <= '9'))
    cout << "This is a digit" << endl ;
else
    cout << "This is not a digit" << endl ;
```

7.4 The switch statement

We now illustrate a further selection construct of C++ by implementing the display_grade function. This will display the calculated grade, a single letter A, B, C, D or E, together with an encouraging message. The way in which the grade is evaluated from the weighted average, as part of the new initialise function, is explained later in this section. Figure 7.6 contains the pseudo-code for the display_grade function.

```
student_marks_2::display_grade
    Call display_identities
    Display the grade letter
    SWITCH on grade letter
        CASE 'A' display 'Excellent'
        CASE 'B' display 'Very good'
        CASE 'C' display 'Pass, but you must try
                                 harder'
        DEFAULT  display 'must try harder'
    Move cursor to the next line
```

Figure 7.6

In this example, we introduce the multi-way selection with the word SWITCH followed by a data item whose value is examined and then determines one of the processing options. The alternative values under consideration are next listed (indented) introduced by the word CASE followed by a statement (or it could be a sequence of statements) to be executed when that value is present. DEFAULT is a special case for all other values not specifically mentioned.

The C++ code for the function display_grade is given in figure 7.7. Note that it contains the C++ selection construct switch. This is the code we use when we want to select one of several different courses of action depending on the value of a single expression, in this case the single character grade_letter. Using switch, the desired course of action is selected immediately after a single inspection of the value of grade_letter.

Following the keyword switch, we have an expression in parentheses that must give an integer value or, as above, a character value. There follows, enclosed within braces, any number of **case groups**. A case group consists of the keyword case followed by a possible value of the expression, followed by a colon, followed by one or more statements to be executed if the expression has

```
void student_marks_2::display_grade ()
  {
  display_identities () ;
  cout << "The grade is " << grade_letter << " " ;
  switch (grade_letter)
    {
    case 'A' : cout << "Excellent" ;
               break ;
    case 'B' : cout << "Very good" ;
               break ;
    case 'C' : cout << "Pass, but you " ;
    default  : cout << "must try harder" ;
    }
  cout << endl ;
  }
```

Figure 7.7

the specified value. The case values must all be distinct constants of the same type as the **switch** expression.

The **break** statement is optional. It must be used, however, if we want to prevent the execution "falling through" to the following statements belonging to other case groups. Optionally, as above, the case groups may be followed by a **default** group that specifies one or more statements to be executed if the **switch** expression contains a value not matched in any of the case groups.

The operation flow diagram in figure 7.8 depicts the way in which the tests in this specific example are carried out, and the way in which the presence or absence of the **break** statement affects which statements will be executed. Because there is no **break** at the end of the C group, the **cout** statement associated with the **default** group will also be executed for the C group.

Finally, to complete this development of the student marks example we will describe a new (over-riding) **initialise** function. Here, we will make use of the code in the original initialise function (declared in **marks.h** for the object class **student_marks**) by first calling it and then using additional code to calculate **grade_letter**. In this new code, we will again use the **switch** statement. Figures 7.9 and 7.10 show the pseudo-code and the C++ code.

Notice how we first call the original **initialise** function from the object class **student_marks**.

```
student_marks::initialise () ;
```

We must use the scope resolution operator (**::**) to indicate that the **initialise** function being called is the one defined in section 5.4 (see figure 5.4) for the object class **student_marks** (see figure 5.5).

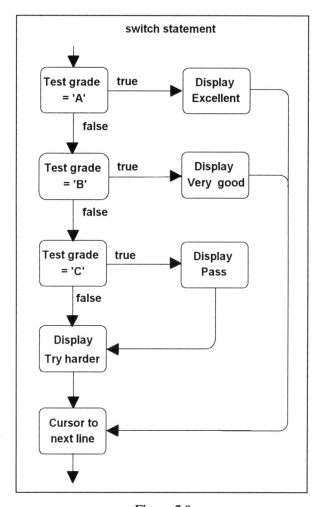

Figure 7.8

The additional code is a **switch** statement. Recall that the expression in parentheses after **switch** must give an integer or character value. But, we are dealing here with a real (**float**) number in **weighted_average**. We must, therefore, convert the real number to integer form by means of a **cast**.

A cast is shown in this statement.

```
switch (int (weighted_average + 0.5) / 10)
```

Here we add 0.5 to **weighted_average** and reinterpret the result as an integer by preceding the parenthesised expression with **int**. We have added 0.5 to round up the weighted average because simply using the **int** cast alone would cause the value to be truncated. This new integer value is then divided by

```
student_marks_2::initialise
   Call student_marks::initialise
   SWITCH on weighted average divided by 10
      CASE 7, 8, 9, 10 : set grade letter = 'A'
      CASE 6           : set grade letter = 'B'
      CASE 5           : set grade letter = 'C'
      CASE 4           : set grade letter = 'D'
      DEFAULT          : set grade letter = 'E'
```

Figure 7.9

```
void student_marks_2::initialise ()
   {
   student_marks::initialise () ;
   switch (int (weighted_average + 0.5) / 10)
      {
      case 10 : ;
      case 9  : ;
      case 8  : ;
      case 7  : grade_letter = 'A' ;
                break ;
      case 6  : grade_letter = 'B' ;
                break ;
      case 5  : grade_letter = 'C' ;
                break ;
      case 4  : grade_letter = 'D' ;
                break ;
      default : grade_letter = 'E' ;
      }
   }
```

Figure 7.10

10 to give a value between 0 and 10 which is now used as the basis of the `switch` statement.

For example, suppose the weighted average is 39.6.

```
weighted_average + 0.5 is 40.1
int (weighted_average + 0.5) is 40
int (weighted_average + 0.5) / 10 is 4
```

and the corresponding case group then assigns 'D' to `grade_letter`.

This example illustrates how several constant values may be placed in front of the same statement. This is used when the same action is to be taken for several different selected values.

```
case 10 : ;
case 9  : ;
case 8  : ;
case 7  : grade_letter = 'A' ;
           break ;
```

In our case, as all weighted averages of at least 69.5% attract a grade A, a revised integer value of 10, 9, 8 or 7 should get grade A. So, we have the first three of these values with no statement (just the colon and semicolon) so that in each of these cases execution will "fall through" to the statement for **case 7**.

Notice the last 3 lines of the **switch** statement.

```
case 4     : grade_letter = 'D' ;
             break ;
default    : grade_letter = 'E' ;
```

All values below 4 are dealt with by the **default** case, hence getting a grade E.

7.5 Exercises

7.5.1 Please refer to the example in figure 7.5, then answer the following questions:

(a) Give the three logical operators in their order of precedence.

(b) In line 9, which parentheses are a mandatory part of C++ and which are not? Why are extra parentheses sometimes used?

(c) What is the not equals (or inequality) operator?

(d) Refer to line 16 and explain how the negation operator works.

7.5.2 Write an **if-else** statement that would display an appropriate message depending on whether or not the value held in **grade_letter** is in fact a valid grade (see section 7.3).

7.5.3 Please refer to the example in figure 7.7, then answer the following questions:

(a) What is the type of **grade_letter** and what values may be contained in a data item of this type?

(b) The expression following the keyword **switch** must give what kind of value?

(c) What are the components of a case group?

(d) What is the effect of a **break** statement?

(e) What is the effect of a **default** statement?

(f) What would be displayed on the monitor screen for a grade B, a grade C and a grade D?

7.5.4 Please refer to the example in figure 7.10, then answer the following questions:

(a) What effect does the expression of the **switch** statement give? What is the resultant value when **weighted_average** is 23.2, 46.5 and 79.5? What are the corresponding values for **grade_letter**?

(b) What happens if a case group contains no statement, as in lines 6, 7 and 8?

7.5.5   Produce a header file (**marks75.h**) that inherits **student_marks_2** from **marks2.h**, incorporating one new function **display_average**, and a program file (**assign75.cpp**) to achieve the following specification.

Prompt the user of the program to enter the identities and the examination and practical marks, then display the results of testing for zero marks (as before). Then call a function, **display_average**, which uses the inherited data item **sum**; provided the **sum** is not zero the average is displayed with appropriate text, otherwise just an appropriate message is displayed.

7.5.6   Produce a header file (**marks76.h**) that inherits **student_marks_2** from **marks2.h** and a program file (**assign76.cpp**) to achieve the following specification. Write the pseudo-code for **initialise** before writing the C++ code.

Prompt the user of the program to enter the identities and the two marks then display the grade (as before). Redefine the **initialise** function to calculate a grade of A if both the exam and practical mark are at least 75%, B for both marks between 50% and 74% inclusive and C otherwise.

7.5.7   Produce a header file (**convert.h**) and a program file (**assign77.cpp**) to achieve the following specification.

A program is required to convert a number, in the range 1 to 100, to its equivalent single character representation in Roman numerals. Any number not capable of this simple conversion or outside the valid range is reported as an error. The user enters the number at the keyboard. The dialogue on the screen will have the form

```
Enter number 5
5 gives the Roman numeral V
```
or
```
Enter number 7
7 cannot be converted
```

The model is shown as an object schema in figure 7.11 and the pseudo-code in figure 7.12 for the member functions and figure 7.13 for the main program.

```
                    Class : convert

                number
                roman numeral

                Get number
                Convert to Roman numeral
                Display Roman numeral
```

Figure 7.11

```
convert::get_number
   Declare terminator variable
   Prompt for and accept number

convert::convert_to_roman_numeral
   SWITCH on number
       CASE 1    : set roman numeral = 'I'
       CASE 5    : set roman numeral = 'V'
       CASE 10   : set roman numeral = 'X'
       CASE 50   : set roman numeral = 'L'
       CASE 100  : set roman numeral = 'C'
       DEFAULT   : set roman numeral = '?'

convert::display_roman_numeral
   Display number
   IF roman numeral is a question mark
      Display error message
   ELSE
      Display text and roman numeral
```

Figure 7.12

```
main
   Declare dial of type convert
   Call dial.get_number
   Call dial.convert_to_roman_numeral
   Call dial.display_roman_numeral
```

Figure 7.13

8 Repetition

Objectives for this chapter
Familiarity with C++ programming terms and concepts:
- `while`, `for` and `do-while` constructs
- a declaration with variable initialisation.

Ability to:
- understand a simple C++ program that uses `while`, `for` and `do-while`
- write simple C++ programs that use `while`, `for` and `do-while`
- use the 'read-ahead' technique with the `while` construct
- understand some concepts of data validation
- distinguish the need for the different types of repetition statement
- write pseudo-code using iteration constructs.

8.1 Refining the input processes for the student's marks

We have seen that programming requires the ability to make decisions. Iterations (or repetitions) are used when we need to repeat actions either a certain number of times or until a pre-determined condition has been reached. The statements to be repeated are sometimes known as loops, and the process of repetition as looping.

We can illustrate the way in which program statements can be repeated a number of times by developing the student's marks example still further. Suppose that both the practical mark and the examination mark have to be calculated from a number of component marks and that the computer user enters these marks one value at a time.

We will need to write a new `initialise` function to accomplish this revised specification. To simplify matters, we will specify this so that it calls `get_identities`, `get_practical_mark`, `get_exam_mark` and `do_calculations`. The new class definition inherits `student_marks_2`, its derivation is depicted in the object schema in figure 8.1 and the C++ code from `marks2A.h` is shown in figure 8.2.

The function `get_identities` prompts for and accepts the module and student identity. The function `do_calculations` calculates the sum of the exam mark and practical mark, the weighted average and the grade letter.

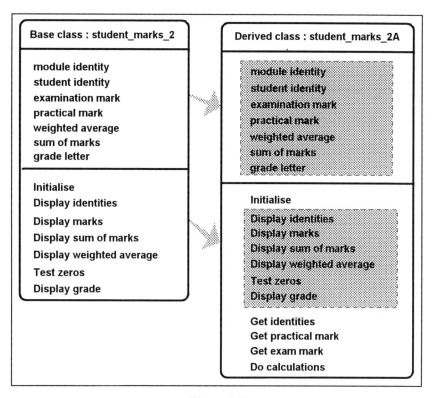

Figure 8.1

```
// MARKS2A.H
// The object class student_marks_2A
#include "marks2.h"
class student_marks_2A : public student_marks_2
    {
    public :
        void get_identities () ;
        void get_practical_mark () ;
        void get_exam_mark () ;
        void do_calculations () ;
        void initialise () ;
    } ;
```

Figure 8.2

The `initalise` function (given in figure 8.3) is simply a sequence of function calls. The functions `get_identities` (given in figure 8.4) and `do_calculations` (in figure 8.5) are simply extracts from previous versions of `initialise`.

```
void student_marks_2A::initialise ()
   {
   get_identities () ;
   get_exam_mark () ;
   get_practical_mark () ;
   do_calculations () ;
   }
```

Figure 8.3

```
void student_marks_2A::get_identities ()
   {
   char terminator ;
   cout << "Enter student identity code " ;
   cin.get (student_identity, 9) ;
   cin.get (terminator) ;
   cout << "Enter module identity code " ;
   cin.get (module_identity, 6) ;
   cin.get (terminator) ;
   }
```

Figure 8.4

```
void student_marks_2A::do_calculations ()
   {
   const float exam_weight = 0.75,
               practical_weight = 0.25 ;
   sum = exam_mark + practical_mark ;
   weighted_average = exam_mark * exam_weight +
      practical_mark * practical_weight ;
   switch (int (weighted_average + 0.5) / 10)
      {
      case 10   : ;
      case 9    : ;
      case 8    : ;
      case 7    : grade_letter = 'A' ;
                  break ;
      case 6    : grade_letter = 'B' ;
                  break ;
      case 5    : grade_letter = 'C' ;
                  break ;
      case 4    : grade_letter = 'D' ;
                  break ;
      default   : grade_letter = 'E' ;
      }
   }
```

Figure 8.5

8.2 The while statement

We will now develop the function **get_practical_mark** with the specification that a student's practical mark is the average of a variable number of component marks. The computer user enters these component marks one value at a time and signifies the end of the list of values by typing the impossibly high mark 999. The pseudo-code for **get_practical_mark** is given in figure 8.6.

```
student_marks_2A::get_practical_mark
   Declare variables
   Initialise number of component marks (= 0)
   Initialise total practical mark (= 0)
   Prompt for and get first practical component mark
      (or 999)
   WHILE practical component mark not 999
      Add component mark to total practical mark
      Increase number of component marks by 1
      Prompt for and get next practical component
         mark (or 999)
   Skip over final newline character
   IF number of component marks > 0
      Compute average practical mark
   ELSE
      Practical mark is zero
```

Figure 8.6

In this pseudo-code, we have a sequence of seven components: four elementary operations followed by a **WHILE** construct, then another elementary operation followed by an **IF-ELSE** construct. The **WHILE** construct gives us the ability to repeat a number of operations, in a loop, as long as a particular condition remains true. The operations to be repeated, three in figure 8.6, are indented under the **WHILE** which describes the appropriate condition. We do not know in advance how many times we are to repeat the loop and as the condition may never be true, the operations in the loop may never be executed. Thus we say that the **WHILE** is an indeterminate iteration construct.

The C++ code for get_**practical_mark** is given in figure 8.7

The fundamental repetitive control structure in C++, **while**, is used in figure 8.7 to control the input of practical component marks. Let us consider just this part of the code.

A component mark is obtained; if the mark is not 999 the repetition starts. The four statements (in the compound statement) that accumulate the total practical mark, count the number of component marks that make up the practical mark and obtain the next component mark are executed repeatedly while the component mark is not = 999. When a component mark of 999 is

```
void student_marks_2A::get_practical_mark ()
  {
  char terminator ;
  int  component_mark ;
  int  no_of_marks = 0 ;
  int  total_practical_mark = 0 ;
  cout << "Enter first practical mark (or 999) " ;
  cin >> component_mark ;
  while (component_mark != 999)
     {
     total_practical_mark += component_mark ;
     ++ no_of_marks ;
     cout << "Enter next practical mark (or 999) " ;
     cin >> component_mark ;
     }
  cin.get (terminator) ;
  if (no_of_marks > 0)
     practical_mark = total_practical_mark /
        no_of_marks ;
  else
     practical_mark = 0 ;
  }
```

Figure 8.7

reached, the repetition stops and the next statement is obeyed.

The statement that accumulates the practical mark by adding the component mark uses the **+=** operator; this allows a shorthand expression as seen above for:

```
total_practical_mark = total_practical_mark +
   component_mark ;
```

The condition (relational expression) of the **while** statement must be enclosed within parentheses, and must give a true result for the associated compound statement to be obeyed.

It must also eventually give a false result (that is, not true), otherwise we would have a situation in which the loop would continue an infinite number of times. Hence, the statement to be repeated should eventually do something to make the condition false, as in the example above, where a mark of 999 must eventually be obtained.

If the condition is false when it is first tested, the loop will not be executed. In the above example, if the first mark obtained was 999, the four statements would not be executed, so nothing would be added to **total_practical_mark** and **no_of_marks** would not be increased (they would both remain as zero).

The way in which the `while` loop operates in general is depicted in the operation flow diagram given in figure 8.8.

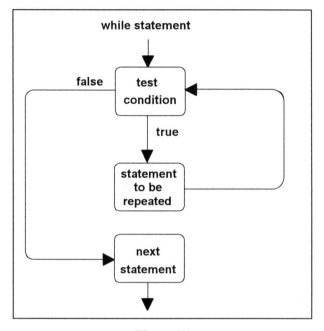

Figure 8.8

An important technique for processing a list of values terminated by a special 'end' value is the so-called 'read-ahead technique'. This is illustrated in the generalised pseudo-code given in figure 8.9.

```
Initialisation (totals and counters to zero)
Get the first value
WHILE continuing condition (value not 'end' value)
    Process the current value
    Get next value
```

Figure 8.9

Using this technique, we must get a value before we can test whether or not we have reached the special 'end' value. This means that we must get a value before entering the loop and we must get the next value as soon as the current value has been processed within the loop. This technique ensures that a program will be correct even when the sequence of values contains only the special 'end' value.

Before we leave this example, there are two further programming features that must be explained. First, note the following declaration.

```
int no_of_marks = 0 ;
```

Here we have declared an integer variable, but at the same time assigned to it the initial value zero. The value of the variable will, under normal circumstances, change as the statements of the function are executed. It should therefore not bc confused with the value given in a constant declaration where the value remains unchanged throughout the execution of the function that owns it.

Now, recall the if-else statement that followed the while loop.

```
if (no_of_marks > 0)
    practical_mark = total_practical_mark /
        no_of_marks ;
else
    practical_mark = 0 ;
```

This statement is necessary in case the while loop is not entered, and hence no_of_marks is never increased from its initial value of zero. Division by zero is not possible and in C++, as with most other programming languages, if there is an attempt to do so, the program will stop with a run-time error. Note also that **practical_mark** was declared as a member data item in the original base class definition, so we must not declare it in this function.

8.3 The for statement

Let us now suppose that, in our example, the examination paper has five questions and the examination mark is calculated by adding together these five marks. The pseudo-code for the function **get_exam_mark** that obtains the five marks and calculates the exam mark is shown in figure 8.10

```
student_marks_2A::get_exam_mark
   Declare variables
   Initialise exam mark (= 0)
   FOR question number from 1 to 5 in steps of 1
       Prompt for and get an exam question mark
       Add exam question mark to exam mark
   Skip over final newline character
```

Figure 8.10

In this pseudo-code we have a sequence of four components. Two elementary operations are followed by a FOR construct then another elementary operation. The FOR construct gives us the ability to repeat, in a loop, a number of operations a pre-determined number of times. Often we may use a counter to control the number of times the loop is repeated. In this case the counter is **question number** and we specify the starting and ending values of the counter as well as the step value. The operations to be repeated, two in figure 8.10, are indented under the **FOR**.

The C++ code for **get_exam_mark** is given in figure 8.11.

```
void student_marks_2A::get_exam_mark ()
  {
  char terminator ;
  int   question_mark ;
  exam_mark = 0 ;
  for (int question_number = 1 ; question_number
     <= 5 ; ++ question_number)
     {
     cout << "Enter examination mark no. " <<
        question_number << " " ;
     cin >> question_mark ;
     exam_mark += question_mark ;
     }
  cin.get (terminator) ;
  }
```

Figure 8.11

This type of repetition, where there is always an expression to be obeyed before entering the loop (**question_number** initialised to 1), a controlling expression (**question_number** is less than or equal to 5), and an expression that is to be obeyed at the end of each loop (increase the value of **question_number** by 1) is very common. For this reason it is catered for by a specific language construct: the **for** statement.

Notice that following the keyword **for**, we have the three components using **question_number** (that is, the expression to be obeyed before entering the loop, the controlling expression, and the expression to be obeyed at the end of each loop). In the first expression, in this case, we declare the integer variable at the same time as giving it an initial value.

The effect of the **for** statement in figure 8.11 is to repeat the associated compound statement, first with **question_number** equal to 1, then 2, then 3, then 4 and finally 5.

We illustrate the way in which the **for** statement operates in the operation flow diagram shown in figure 8.12.

The general form of the **for** statement can be written as:

```
for (expression-1 ; expression-2 ; expression-3)
   statement ;
```

which can be explained by the following equivalent code using **while**:

```
expression-1 ;
while (expression-2)
```

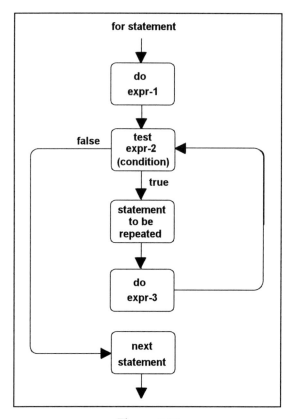

Figure 8.12

```
{
statement ;
expression-3 ;
}
```

This implies that the **while** statement could be used instead of any **for** statement. But the **for** statement should be used whenever we have a count-controlled loop – that is a counter (**question_number** in our case) going from an initial value (1 in our case) to a final value (5 in our case) in steps (1 in our case).

8.4 The do-while statement

The **do-while** statement is another loop control statement. Unlike the **while** and **for** statements, it tests for another repetition at the bottom of the loop instead of the top. This means that the statement to be repeated is executed at least once. The concept is illustrated in the operation flow diagram in figure 8.13.

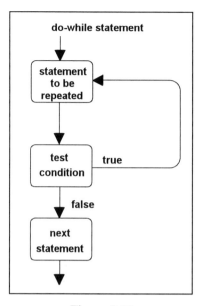

Figure 8.13

As with `while` and `for`, several statements enclosed in braces to form a compound statement, may be placed inside the loop.

The `do-while` statement makes explicit the fact that the loop is always executed at least once and should be used when the loop has to be executed once before the condition can be tested. This often occurs in an interactive dialogue where the user input is validated to be correct. For example, in our student's marks example, if each question is marked out of 20, we should really insist that any examination question mark entered lies in the range 0 to 20.

A new version of `get_exam_mark`, incorporating a `do-while` statement to validate the input, is shown in pseudo-code in figure 8.14.

```
student_marks_2A::get_exam_mark
   Declare variables
   Initialise exam mark (= 0)
   FOR question number from 1 to 5 in steps of 1
      DO
           Prompt for and get an exam question mark
      WHILE exam question mark is invalid
      Add exam question mark to exam mark
   Skip over final newline character
```

Figure 8.14

In this pseudo-code we have an initial sequence of four components. Two elementary operations are followed by a **FOR** construct then another elementary operation. The **FOR** statement will repeat a sequence of two operations: a **DO-WHILE** construct followed by an elementary operation. In this case there is only one operation to be repeated in the loop; this is indented under the **DO**.

The C++ code for this version of **get_exam_mark** is given in figure 8.15.

```
void student_marks_2A::get_exam_mark ()
   {
   char terminator ;
   int  question_mark ;
   exam_mark = 0 ;
   for (int question_number = 1 ; question_number
      <= 5 ; ++ question_number)
      {
      do
         {
         cout << "Enter examination mark no. " <<
            question_number << " " ;
         cin >> question_mark ;
         }
      while (! ((question_mark >= 0) &&
         (question_mark <= 20))) ;
      exam_mark += question_mark ;
      }
   cin.get (terminator) ;
   }
```

Figure 8.15

The validation is achieved by repeatedly asking the user to input a mark until a valid mark is entered (that is, it is in the required range) or, to put it another way, while the user continues to enter an invalid mark.

Notice that the condition for continuing the inner loop:

```
while (! ((question_mark >= 0) &&
   (question_mark <= 20))) ;
```

can only be evaluated once the user has entered a mark. Hence we have to test the condition at the end of the loop and need a repetition of at least one occurrence.

8.5 Exercises

8.5.1 Please refer to the example in figure 8.7, then answer the following questions:

(a) How many times would the statements in the `while` loop be executed if the user of the program typed in 999 as the first practical component mark?

(b) Which statement is executed next after the `while` when the value of `component_mark` is 999?

(c) What would happen if the second `cin >> component_mark` was omitted?

(d) If the user typed in 50 then 60 then 999 for the practical mark components, what would be contained in the variables `no_of_marks`, `total_practical_mark` and `component_mark` after completion of the `while` loop?

(e) Why is the `if` statement necessary?

8.5.2 Please refer to the example in figure 8.11, then answer the following questions:

(a) How many times is the first expression of the `for` statement executed?

(b) How many times is the third expression of the `for` statement executed?

(c) If the number of examination questions was reduced to four, what statements would need to be changed?

(d) Why do we not use the read-ahead technique in this example?

(e) What changes would you make to rewrite the code in this example using a `while` statement instead of the `for` statement. Which is better, this code or that given in the example? Give your reasoning.

(f) If `question_number` was initialised to 0 rather than 1, what effect would this have on the way we would code the relational expression in the `for` statement?

8.5.3 Please refer to the example in figure 8.15, then answer the following questions:

(a) Why must there be at least one repetition of the statements in a `do-while` loop?

(b) What is the purpose of the `do-while` loop in this example?

(c) Write alternative code for the `do_while` loop using a `while` loop. Is this code better or worse than that given in the example? Give your reasoning.

(d) What changes would you make if the number of questions is reduced to four with 25 marks for each question?

(e) For this revised specification, rewrite the compound condition for the while using **| |** rather than **!** and **&&**. Hint: for which values is the mark invalid?

8.5.4   Produce a header file (**marks84.h**) that inherits **student_marks_2A** from **marks2A.h** and incorporates new versions of **get_exam_mark** and **initialise**. Produce appropriate pseudo-code for these two functions before coding them.

The revised version of **get_exam_mark** calculates the exam mark by adding together an unknown number of examination question marks (so there is no need to validate these marks). The user is prompted for and enters a mark one value at a time and indicates that there are no more by typing a -1.

The revised version of **initialise** must include all existing features and validate the exam mark by ensuring that it is greater than the practical mark.

8.5.5   Produce a header file (**triang.h**) and a program file (**assign85.cpp**) to achieve the specification described by the object schema in figure 8.16 and the pseudo-code in figure 8.17 for the member functions and figure 8.18 for the main program.

You should use prompts that ask for the dimensions in centimetres and display the result to 2 decimal places with appropriate text.

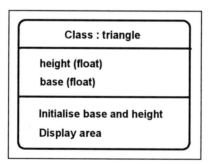

Figure 8.16

```
triangle::initialise
   Declare terminator variable
   DO
      Prompt for and accept height
   WHILE height < 10.0
   DO
      Prompt for and accept base
   WHILE base < 12.5
   Skip over final newline character

triangle::display_area
   Declare area variable
   Calculate area (height * base / 2)
   Display area
```

Figure 8.17

```
main
   Declare example of type triangle
   FOR counter from 1 to 6 in steps of 1
      Call example.initialise
      Call example.display_area
```

Figure 8.18

9 Functions

Objectives for this chapter

Familiarity with C++ programming terms and concepts:
- function calls and definitions
- formal and actual parameters
- function results
- private member functions
- the `return` statement
- call by value and call by reference, alias parameters
- the address operator `&`
- integer values as true or false.

Ability to:
- understand the use of functions with both call by value and call by reference parameters
- write simple C++ programs that use functions with call by value and call by reference parameters.

9.1 The function call

In all the previous examples, we have implemented the behaviour of objects by writing member functions. Such functions have then been invoked or called by statements such as

```
initialise () ;
```

or for instances of an object by statements such as

```
history.test_first_class_mark () ;
```

In such cases, the function call exists as an executable statement with no arguments. The effect of the call is to cause the statements of the function to be executed; when completed, the calling function or program continues from the next statement.

We have also used functions provided by C++ in standard libraries. For example, we called the function `strcpy` found in `<string.h>` by

```
strcpy (contents, "Hello World") ;
```

Again, the function call exists as an executable statement but now it has two arguments. The effect of the call is to cause the statements of the function to be executed, that is, the string **"Hello World"** is copied into **contents**. Thus the second argument is supplied to the function and does not have its value changed by the function. The first argument, however, does have its value changed by the function call.

A full range of mathematical functions is available in **<math.h>**. For example we could call the **pow** (power) function as follows

```
volume = 3.14 * pow (radius, 2) * height ;
```

The function **pow** takes two arguments. In this case, **radius** (a value to be raised by a power) and **2** (the power used). It returns the result **radius^2**. The function call appears in an expression and after execution is replaced by the returned value.

We could also call the **sqrt** (square root) function as in the following statement

```
sides = sqrt ((height * height) + (width * width)) ;
```

The function **sqrt** takes a single argument (an expression that gives a value of type **double**) and returns a result of type **double** (**double** is an extended form of type **float**). Here, the function call has a single value and appears on the right-hand side of an assignment statement, but it could equally well have been part of an expression. The effect of the call is to pass the value of the argument (an expression in this case) to the function, which executes and returns the square root of that value as the result of the function. The result is then assigned to **sides**.

Thus a function can return a value either by changing one of its parameters or as the result of the function. Note that C++ allows for all functions to return a result value as well as the possibility of having arguments whose values may or may not be changed.

9.2 The function definition

As we have seen, a function is a self-contained subprogram that can be called (invoked) from a main program or another subprogram. These functions are either held in C++ libraries or defined in the program or header file by a function definition. This consists of the function heading followed by the statements that belong to the function enclosed in braces, known as the body of the function. Hence the general form of a function definition is:

```
result_type function_identifier (parameter_list)
    {
    statements
    }
```

In fact, a main program is itself a function. Recall that we have started the executable part of our programs with **void main ()** which is a function heading with no result type, as indicated by **void**, and an empty parameter (argument) list.

9.3 A revised version of the student marks object class

Let us now develop a different version of the **student_marks** object class to illustrate the use of function definitions with parameters and result values and the way functions are called. We will again use **student_marks_2** as the base class, this time introducing both new and overriding member functions as well as three new private functions. The derivation of the new object class is depicted in the object schema given in figure 9.1 and the C++ code for the new class definition is given in figure 9.2.

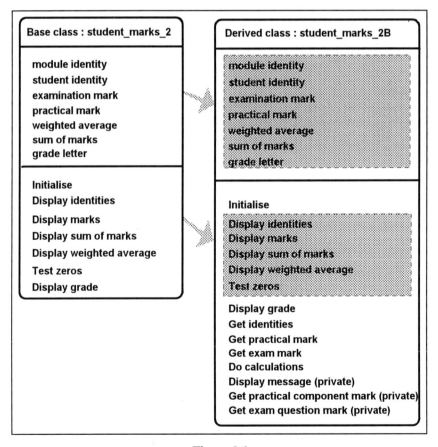

Figure 9.1

```
// MARKS2B.H
// The object class student_marks_2B
#include "marks2.h"
class student_marks_2B : public student_marks_2
   {
   public :
      void initialise () ;
      void get_identities () ;
      void display_grade () ;
      void get_practical_mark () ;
      void get_exam_mark () ;
      void do_calculations () ;
   private :
      void display_message (const char* message) ;
      int get_practical_component_mark (const
         char* title) ;
      int get_exam_question_mark (int question_no,
         int& mark) ;
   } ;
```

Figure 9.2

The three member functions initialise, get_identities and do_calculations are coded as in student_marks_2A (see figures 8.3, 8.4 and 8.5). The new function display_grade uses the private function display_message, get_practical_mark uses the private function get_practical_component_mark and get_exam_mark uses the private function get_exam_question_mark. The private functions may only be used within functions of the same class.

We will describe the new functions to illustrate various features of function definitions, parameters and results.

9.4 Call by value parameters

First note the format of the first private function prototype.

```
void display_message (const char* message) ;
```

The result type is void, indicating that the function does not return a result value. The function identifier is display_message and there is one parameter specified as const char* message which allows a string of characters to be used, but not changed, by the function. Formally, char* means that the parameter is of a type known as a pointer to a char; we will consider pointers in chapter 14. The constant reference const indicates that the contents of the argument will not be changed by the function. The identifier

```
void student_marks_2B::display_message (const
   char* message)
   {
   cout << "Well done " << student_identity
      << " you have obtained a grade "
      << grade_letter << endl ;
   cout << "This is a " << message << " result"
      << endl ;
   }
```

Figure 9.3

message gives a name to the parameter.

Now let us consider the function definition for **display_message**, this is given in figure 9.3. The first line of the function definition is the function header.

```
void student_marks_2B::display_message (const
   char* message)
```

This contains the result type **void** followed by the function name (including the class identifier and the scope resolution operator) **student_marks_2B::display_message** followed by the parameter list in parentheses. In this case, the parameter list contains only one entry defining a **const char*** parameter called **message**. Any parameter used in the function definition, such as **message** in this case, is known as a formal parameter. Notice that the header matches the prototype in terms of the result type, function name and number and type of parameters.

The code in braces is referred to as the body of the function. In this case it consists of two **cout** statements. The second statement uses the value of the parameter **message**; it is sent to the output stream by **cout**.

Since **display_message** has a single formal parameter, it must be invoked by a function call containing a single expression of the appropriate type as its argument. In the revised function **display_grade**, given as figure 9.4, we see four calls to **display_message**. One of the calls is

```
display_message ("very good") ;
```

This is a function call to the function **display_message** with the argument **"very good"**. Any argument used in the function call is known as an actual parameter. The C++ code in the body of the function definition for **display_message** is now executed with the value of the actual parameter, **"very good"**, being substituted for the formal parameter, **message**. This results in **"very good"** being displayed as part of a standard line of output:

```
This is a very good result
```

```
void student_marks_2B::display_grade ()
   {
   switch (grade_letter)
      {
      case 'A'  : display_message ("superb") ;
                  break ;
      case 'B'  : display_message ("very good") ;
                  break ;
      case 'C'  : display_message ("reasonable") ;
                  break ;
      default   : display_message ("weak") ;
      }
   }
```

Figure 9.4

This example illustrates one advantage of using functions in that **display_message** is used four times in **display_grade** but without having to repeat the C++ code given in the definition of **display_message**. It also demonstrates the purpose of a parameter. By using the formal parameter **message** in the function definition, we are then able to substitute different actual values at each call..

As we have seen in previous chapters, a function does not necessarily have to have parameters. The parameters are then said to be void. For example, we have used a function call of the form

```
initialise () ;
```

The function prototype and definition heading is then of the form

```
void initialise (void)
```

or

```
void initialise ()
```

9.5 Function results

So far we have defined only functions that have a **void** result although we did briefly describe the use of functions such as **sqrt** that do return a result. To return a result after the execution of a function, the function must use the keyword **return**.

Consider the private function **get_practical_component_mark** prototyped in figure 9.2 by:

```
int get_practical_component_mark (const char* title) ;
```

In this function, we repeatedly prompt for a practical component mark

```
student_marks_2B::get_practical_component_mark
   (title)
   Declare mark variable
   DO
       Prompt for a mark
       Get a mark from keyboard
   WHILE mark not valid (i.e. not 0-100,999)
   Return valid mark
```

Figure 9.5

```
int student_marks_2B::get_practical_component_mark
   (const char* title)
   {
   int  mark ;
   do
       {
       cout << "Enter " << title
           << " practical mark (or 999) " ;
       cin >> mark ;
       }
   while (! ((mark >= 0) && (mark <= 100)
       || (mark == 999))) ;
   return mark ;
   }
```

Figure 9.6

until a mark in the valid range of 0 to 100 or 999 is entered at the keyboard. The parameter is used to provide either the string **"first"** or **"next"** for use within the prompt. The valid mark is returned as the **int** result of the function. The pseudo-code for this function is given in figure 9.5 and the C++ code in figure 9.6.

We note that the function header has both a parameter and a result type:

```
int student_marks_2B::get_practical_component_mark
   (const char* title)
```

The parameter is of a similar form to that used in **display_message**. The function result is defined by the **int** preceding the function identifier. This indicates that before the execution of the function is completed some integer value must be returned as the function's result. In this example a valid practical component mark value (or the end marker 999) is eventually obtained in the **int** variable **mark**. When the function is called this is returned as the function's result by means of **return mark**.

We can illustrate the way in which this function is called by reference to the new member function **get_practical_mark**. This is shown in pseudo-

```
student_marks_2B::get_practical_mark
   Declare variables
   Initialise number of component marks (= 0)
   Initialise total practical mark (= 0)
   Call get_practical_component_mark
   WHILE practical component mark not 999
      Add component mark to total practical mark
      Increase number of component marks by 1
      Call get_practical_component_mark
   Skip over final newline character
   IF number of component marks > 0
      Compute average practical mark
   ELSE
      Practical mark is zero
```

Figure 9.7

```
void student_marks_2B::get_practical_mark ()
   {
   char terminator ;
   int component_mark ;
   int no_of_marks = 0 ;
   int total_practical_mark = 0 ;
   component_mark = get_practical_component_mark
      ("first") ;
   while (component_mark != 999)
      {
      total_practical_mark += component_mark ;
      ++ no_of_marks ;
      component_mark = get_practical_component_mark
         ("next") ;
      }
   cin.get (terminator) ;
   if (no_of_marks > 0)
      practical_mark = total_practical_mark /
         no_of_marks ;
   else
      practical_mark = 0 ;
   }
```

Figure 9.8

code form as figure 9.7 and in C++ code in figure 9.8. This is very similar to the function described in the previous chapter. The only difference is that we now use the function calls:

```
component_mark = get_practical_component_mark
   ("first") ;
```

and

```
component_mark = get_practical_component_mark
    ("next") ;
```

In both instances the argument is passed to the function and substituted for the formal parameter `title` to produce the appropriate prompt; a valid mark is returned on completion of the function's execution to be assigned to the variable `component_mark`.

9.6 Call by reference parameters

As we saw in figure 9.4, a function call can pass values to the function by means of one or more parameters. For example

```
display_message ("very good") ;
```

There still remains the problem of how to define and use functions that can be called and will then change the values of some of the arguments such as when using `strcpy`. The answer to this lies in the way in which we specify the formal parameters. An example is provided in the third of our private functions defined in `student_marks_2B`: `get_exam_question_mark` prototyped as

```
int get_exam_question_mark (int question_no,
    int& mark) ;
```

In this function, we check the validity of a mark entered by the user at the keyboard and interpret the mark as an integer value. A valid mark consists solely of the digits between 0 and 9 and its value must be less than or equal to the maximum mark of 20 for an examination question. The first parameter passes across the question number for use in a prompt. The value of this parameter will not be changed by the function, but as will be explained in the next section there is no need to include `const` as we did with `char*`. The second parameter is used to return the mark.

The function will return a result value of 1 for valid input and 0 for invalid input. If the user enters 17, 1 is returned as the function result and 17 is delivered as the value of the second parameter. If, for example, the user enters any of 3.7, 4A2 or 28, 0 is returned as both the function result and the value of the second parameter.

Note that in the second parameter after the type `int` there follows the address operator `&` (ampersand). This indicates that the formal parameter will be used as an **alias** of the actual parameter. How does this work?

Let us examine the function definition given as pseudo-code in figure 9.9 and C++ in figure 9.10.

First, we will describe the function header.

```
int student_marks_2B::get_exam_question_mark
    (int question_no, int& mark)
```

```
student_marks_2B::get_exam_question_mark
   (question_no, mark)
   Declare variable
   Initialise error indicator and mark (= 0)
   Prompt for an examination question mark
   Get a character
   WHILE current character is not end of line
      IF current character is a digit
          Multiply current mark by 10
          Add current character's value to mark
      ELSE
          Set error indicator = 1
      Get next character
   IF mark > 20 or error indicator = 1
      Set mark to 0
      Return 0 (invalid)
   ELSE
      Return 1 (valid)
```

Figure 9.9

```
int student_marks_2B::get_exam_question_mark
   (int question_no, int& mark)
   {
   char character ;
   int error_indicator = 0 ;
   mark = 0 ;
   cout << "Enter examination mark no. "
      << question_no << " " ;
   cin.get (character) ;
   while (character != '\n')
      {
      if ((character >= '0') && (character <= '9'))
         {
         mark *= 10 ;
         mark += character - 48 ;
         }
      else
          error_indicator = 1 ;
      cin.get (character) ;
      }
   if ((mark > 20) || (error_indicator == 1))
      {
      mark = 0 ;
      return 0 ;
      }
   else
      return 1 ;
   }
```

Figure 9.10

As with the prototype, again notice the address operator (**&**) associated with the second type **int** and formal parameter **mark** in the parameter list. If the address operator is added to the end of the data type this indicates that the formal parameter is to be regarded as an **alias** of the actual parameter. This means that when such a function is called, instead of simply using the value contained in an actual parameter, the function uses the actual parameter itself. Hence, when we specify a formal parameter in this way we allow the value of its corresponding actual parameter to be changed by the function.

When **get_exam_question_mark** is called, for example in

```
valid_mark = get_exam_question_mark
     (question_number, question_mark) ;
```

The value of the **mark** obtained in the function is placed directly into **question_mark** because **mark** is being used as an alias for **question_mark**.

In the function definition, having declared a **char** variable called **character**, initialised **error_indicator** and the parameter **mark** to zero, then displayed the prompt, we use the read-ahead technique and obtain the first character from the keyboard using **cin.get (character)**.

Next we use a **while** statement to obtain a character at a time until the end of line character has been recognised. Notice, first, the way the loop is controlled.

```
while (character != '\n')
```

We use this form of loop because we will allow for the possibility of having an 'empty' number entered, that is just the end of line character. End of line is indicated in C++ code using the special character constant '\n'.

If the character we are currently processing is a digit (in the range 0 to 9), then we add it to the mark so far, taking into account the position of the digit; otherwise we set the **error_indicator** to 1.

```
if ((character >= '0') && (character <= '9'))
     {
     mark *= 10 ;
     mark += character - 48 ;
     }
else
     error_indicator = 1 ;
cin.get (character) ;
```

So, if the **character** is a digit, we multiply the current value of **mark** by 10, the ***=** operator allows the above shorthand for **mark = mark * 10**, then add to it the digit value of **character**. In this latter operation, it is necessary to subtract 48 from the value of **character** to convert it from the character representation of a number to the number itself. This may seem a strange concept subtracting a numeric value from a character, but recall (see section

7.3) that each character has an equivalent numeric value, hence C++ allows such arithmetic. We then have the next read ahead: `cin.get (character)`.

Let us explain the two arithmetic assignments using some sample data. We will use the data **157\n** (entered by typing 157 then pressing the enter key). We enter the while loop with **character** containing the character value '1' which is the numeric value 49 and **mark** containing zero. The table in figure 9.11 traces the changing values of **character** and **mark**.

	character		mark
	character value	numeric value	
On entry to the `while`	'1'	49	0
`mark *= 10`			0
`mark += character - 48`			1
`cin.get (character)`	'5'	53	
`mark *= 10`			10
`mark += character - 48`			15
`cin.get (character)`	'7'	55	
`mark *= 10`			150
`mark += character - 48`			157
`cin.get (character)`	'\n'		

Figure 9.11

Finally, we must return the result of the function.
```
if ((mark > 20) || (error_indicator == 1))
    {
    mark = 0 ;
    return 0 ;
    }
else
    return 1 ;
```
The **return** statement will return a value according to the function type. Recall that our function has a type of **int**. So, if the resultant value of **mark** is greater than 20 (an invalid mark) or the **error_indicator** has been changed from its initial value of zero to 1, as well as setting the value of **mark** to zero, the function returns the value 0, otherwise the value 1 is returned.

The context in which **get_exam_question_mark** is used can be explained with reference to the revised **get_exam_mark** function which is shown in pseudo-code as figure 9.12 and C++ in figure 9.13.

```
student_marks_2B::get_exam_mark
   Declare variables
   Initialise exam mark (= 0)
   FOR question number from 1 to 5 in steps of 1
      DO
         Call get_exam_question_mark
      WHILE not a valid mark
      Add question mark to exam mark
```

Figure 9.12

```
void student_marks_2B::get_exam_mark ()
   {
   int question_mark ;
   int valid_mark ;
   exam_mark = 0 ;
   for (int question_number = 1 ; question_number
      <= 5 ; ++ question_number)
      {
      do
         {
         valid_mark = get_exam_question_mark
            (question_number, question_mark) ;
         }
      while (valid_mark == 0) ;
      exam_mark += question_mark ;
      }
   }
```

Figure 9.13

In this version, we have a declaration for the `int` variable `valid_mark`, which is used in the function call to `get_exam_question_mark` and the relational expression of the `do-while` statement.

```
valid_mark = get_exam_question_mark
      (question_number, question_mark) ;
   }
while (valid_mark == 0) ;
```

After the function `get_exam_question_mark` is called, the previous value of `question_mark` would be replaced by the value computed as `mark` in the function. Also a zero or one would be returned by the function and would be placed in `valid_mark`.

Now, note the use of `valid_mark` in the relational expression of the `while` statement. We have previously explained that a relational expression will either have a value of true or false. In C++, the values true and false are represented by 1 and 0. Alternatively, an integer value of 0 can be interpreted as false and any non-zero integer value as true. So, in this case, if an invalid mark has been obtained in the function, the function returns a zero which is interpreted as false, hence the **do-while** condition could have been coded simply as

```
while (! valid_mark) ;
```

The same technique could also have been used in the function **get_exam_question_mark**

```
if ((mark > 20) || (error_indicator == 1))
```

could have been coded by

```
if ((mark > 20) || error_indicator)
```

9.7 When to use call by value and call by reference

If we merely want to pass a value to a function we use a call by value parameter, if we want a value returned from a function to the actual parameter we use a call by reference.

With call by value, the value of the actual parameter is not changed by the function, because the function uses separate store locations for the actual and formal parameters. With a call by reference (**alias**) parameter, the value of the actual parameter may be changed within the function, because the function refers to the store location of the actual parameter.

For a call by value we normally just give the type as **int, float** etc. in the parameter list of the prototype and function definition. For a call by reference we include the address operator, for example, **int&, float&** etc. In the **display_message** function however, we used **const char*** for a call by value parameter. Because of the way variable length strings are implemented in C++, **char*** by itself would have been interpreted, in effect, as a call by reference.

A function may have some parameters using call by value and some using call by reference as illustrated in **get_exam_question_mark** where the first parameter (**question_no**) is call by value and the second (**mark**) a call by reference.

9.8 Exercises

9.8.1 Please refer to section 9.4, and answer the following questions.

(a) How must a function prototype and a function heading correspond?

(b) How must a function heading and a function call correspond?

(c) In what way does a function prototype and a function header differ?

(d) In the function **display_message**, what type of argument is used?

(e) How is the body of a function delimited?

(f) What is the main advantage of using the function **display_message**?

9.8.2   Please refer to the examples given in figures 9.6 and 9.8, then answer the following questions.

(a) How is the result of a function defined?

(b) What is the purpose of the parameter in the function **get_practical_component_mark**?

(c) What is the purpose of the **return** statement?

(d) Why is a **do-while** loop statement used in the function **get_practical_component_mark**?

(e) How many times and how is the function **get_practical_component_mark** called?

9.8.3   Please refer to the examples given in figures 9.10 and 9.13, then answer the following questions.

(a) If the address operator is added to the type of a function parameter, what does this indicate as to the relationship of the formal and actual parameter?

(b) Why is the statement **mark *= 10** used?

(c) Why is the statement **mark += character - 48** used?

(d) What is the purpose of the **return** statement in this function?

(e) How is the function **get_exam_question_mark** called in **get_exam_mark**?

(f) What would be the effect of calling the function **get_exam_question_mark** when **1A4\n** is entered?

(g) What would be the effect of calling the function **get_exam_question_mark** when **134\n** is entered?

(h) What would be the effect of calling the function **get_exam_question_mark** when only **\n** is entered?

9.8.4   For each of the following, write a suitable function prototype, function heading and function call. For the function calls, write a C++ statement that will process the sum of the integers between 10 and 28.

(a) A function with two parameters to display the sum of all integers within a specified range.

(b) A function with two parameters that returns as its result the sum of all integers within a specified range.

(c) A function with three parameters that returns as the third parameter the sum of all integers within a specified range.

9.8.5   Examine the function definitions given in figure 9.14, then answer the questions below.

```
void swap_items_1 (int& item_one, int& item_two)
    {
    int temp_item = item_one ;
    item_one = item_two ;
    item_two = temp_item ;
    }

void swap_items_2 (int item_one, int item_two)
    {
    int temp_item = item_one ;
    item_one = item_two ;
    item_two = temp_item ;
    }
```

Figure 9.14

(a) What is the effect of the function call `swap_items_1` (`item_a`, `item_b`) when `item_a` contains 5 and `item_b` contains 3?

(b) What is the effect of the function call `swap_items_2` (`item_a`, `item_b`) when `item_a` contains 7 and `item_b` contains 6?

9.8.6 Produce a header file (`calcul.h`) and a program file (`assign96.cpp`) to simulate a simple calculator by producing a dialogue of the following form.

```
Enter first operand 5.2
Enter second operand 7.3
Enter the operator *
5.2 * 7.3 = 37.96
```

You should display the result to 2 decimal places. A valid operand is any number other than zero and a valid operator is + or − or * or /.

The model is given as an object schema in figure 9.15. The pseudo-code is in figure 9.16 for the member functions and figure 9.17 for the main program. The function `get_valid_operand` returns a `float` value as its result and has a single parameter that should be used as the prompt. The function `get_valid_operator` has a single parameter that returns the operator as a single character.

```
                    Class : calculator

             operand 1 (float)
             operand 2 (float)
             arithmetic operator

             Initialise operands and operator
             Display result
             Get valid operand (private)
             Get valid operator (private)
```

Figure 9.15

```
calculator::initialise
   Call get_valid_operand for first operand
   Call get_valid_operand for second operand
   Call get_valid_operator

calculator::get_valid_operand (prompt)
   Declare variables
   DO
      Display prompt
      Get an operand
   WHILE operand = zero
   Skip over final newline character
   Return operand

calculator::get_valid_operator (character)
   Declare terminator variable
   DO
      Display prompt for the operator
      Get a character
      Skip over newline character
   WHILE character is not an operator (+ - * /)

calculator::display_result
   Declare result variable
   SWITCH on operator
      CASE '+' : Compute operand 1 + operand 2
      CASE '-' : Compute operand 1 - operand 2
      CASE '*' : Compute operand 1 * operand 2
      CASE '/' : Compute operand 1 / operand 2
   Display operand 1 operator operand 2 = result
```

Figure 9.16

```
main
    Declare example of type calculator
    Call example.initialise
    Call example.display_result
```

Figure 9.17

10 Constructors and Destructors

Objectives for this chapter

Familiarity with C++ programming terms and concepts:

- the default constructor
- programmer-defined constructors
- default parameters
- the default destructor.

Ability to:

- understand the use of constructors and destructors
- write simple C++ programs that use constructors with and without parameters.

10.1 Constructors

When an instance of an object class is created in a program, memory is reserved for each member data item so that the state of the object, that is the values held in each data area, can be preserved. No memory is reserved for the object's functions since these remain unchanged for every instance of an object class; only one copy, for the whole object class, needs to be in memory. However, the value stored in **module_identity**, say, after the appropriate function calls could be different for each instance of the object class **student_marks_2B**. Hence the need to reserve memory for the data areas.

In all our previous examples, a special function called a **default constructor** is called automatically to reserve memory when each object is created. In addition, a **constructor** may be explicitly defined for an object class by the programmer. This too would be called automatically when each object of the class is created.

A programmer may write one or more constructors for an object class. In this chapter we will consider using only one, but in chapter 16 we will describe the use of more than one constructor for an object class. A constructor written by the programmer may be used for any form of processing. For example, we could usefully use a constructor for initialisation of an object. The advantage of doing this lies in the fact that a constructor does not have to be explicitly called; it is, in effect, a function that is called automatically when an object is created.

Also, the programmer does not need to be concerned with the memory reservation actions of a programmer-defined constructor; this is also done automatically.

We can make a minor revision to the object class **student_marks_2B** to illustrate the use of a constructor. The header file (**marks2ba.h**) using a constructor and a program file (**sum_1.cpp**) are now given for consideration as figures 10.1 and 10.2.

```
// MARKS2BA.H
// The object class student_marks_2Ba using a
// constructor
#include "marks2b.h"
class student_marks_2Ba : public student_marks_2B
    {
    public :
        student_marks_2Ba () ;
    } ;

student_marks_2Ba::student_marks_2Ba ()
    {
    initialise () ;
    }
```

Figure 10.1

```
// SUM_1.CPP
// A program to display the sum of the exam and
// practical marks for 2 students in a single
// subject
#include "marks2ba.h"
void main ()
    {
    student_marks_2Ba geography_JP100 ;
    geography_JP100.display_sum () ;
    student_marks_2Ba geography_MK110 ;
    geography_MK110.display_sum () ;
    }
```

Figure 10.2

In the header file, note how the format of a constructor prototype differs from that of a function prototype.

> **student_marks_2Ba () ;**

There is no result type. Also, the name is that of the object class; a constructor always takes the identity of the class to which it belongs. The constructor heading reflects the same rules. We have then used the **initialise** member function in this programmer-defined constructor.

The simplified main program (**sum_1.cpp**) creates two objects, **geography_JP100** and **geography_MK110**. An example of the screen dialogue when this program is run is given in figure 10.3.

```
Enter student identity code JP100
Enter module identity code GEOG
Enter examination mark no. 1 55
. . .
Enter examination mark no. 5 65
Enter first practical mark (or 999) 75
Enter next practical mark (or 999) 999

Student identity: JP100 for Module: GEOG
Exam mark is 63 Practical mark is 75
The sum of the marks is 138
Enter student identity code MK110
Enter module identity code GEOG
Enter examination mark no. 1 63
. . .
Enter examination mark no. 5 41
Enter first practical mark (or 999) 74
Enter next practical mark (or 999) 999

Student identity: MK110 for Module: GEOG
Exam mark is 55 Practical mark is 74
The sum of the marks is 129
```

Figure 10.3

When the object **geography_JP100** is created, the constructor is executed; this in turn calls **initialise** resulting in the dialogue

```
Enter student identity code JP100
Enter module identity code GEOG
. . .
Enter next practical mark (or 999) 999
```

The next four lines of dialogue are produced by the function **display_sum** for **geography_JP100**.

The whole process is then repeated for the object **geography_MK110**. To achieve the dialogue in figure 10.3 without the constructor, we would have to include **geography_JP100.initialise ()** after the declaration of **geography_JP100** and **geography_MK110.initialise ()** after the declaration of **geography_MK110** in the main program (figure 10.2).

10.2 Constructors with parameters

We can use parameters with a constructor to particularise an object's initialisation. Let us now make a further revision to the object class **student_marks_2B** so that instead of the user providing the student and module identities from the keyboard, this data is supplied from within a main program and displayed on the monitor screen. A new version of the header file and program file (**marks2bb.h** and **sum_2.cpp**) are given in figures 10.4 and 10.5.

```
// MARKS2BB.H
// The object class student_marks_2Bb using a
// constructor with parameters
#include <string.h>
#include "marks2b.h"
class student_marks_2Bb : public student_marks_2B
    {
    public :
        student_marks_2Bb (const char* student_id,
            const char* module_id) ;
    } ;

student_marks_2Bb::student_marks_2Bb (const char*
    student_id, const char* module_id = "MATHS")
    {
    cout << " Module " << module_id << "    Student "
        << student_id << endl ;
    strcpy (module_identity, module_id) ;
    strcpy (student_identity, student_id) ;
    get_exam_mark () ;
    get_practical_mark () ;
    do_calculations () ;
    }
```

Figure 10.4

Let us look more closely at the main parts of the header file. First the constructor prototype.

```
student_marks_2Bb (const char* student_id,
    const char* module_id) ;
```

The constructor prototype now has two parameters: a character string that will be used for the student identity and a character string that will be used for the

```
// SUM_2.CPP
// A program to produce the sum of the exam and
// practical marks for a student in one subject and
// for a different student in another subject
#include "marks2bb.h"
void main ()
   {
   student_marks_2Bb geography_MK110 ("MK110",
      "GEOG") ;
   geography_MK110.display_sum () ;
   student_marks_2Bb maths_JP100 ("JP100") ;
   maths_JP100.display_sum () ;
   }
```

Figure 10.5

module identity.

The constructor heading needs to correspond to the prototype already described.

```
student_marks_2Bb::student_marks_2Bb (const char*
   student_id, const char* module_id = "MATHS")
```

As expected, the constructor heading incorporates the formal parameters `student_id` and `module_id` as strings. But notice also, a new syntax feature; after the usual parameter type and name for the second parameter, we have the equals symbol and a string value. This is a way of defining a default value for a constructor's parameter to be used if no value is supplied when an object is created. In fact, any parameter for a function can have a default value in C++.

The parameters from the constructor are used in the `cout` statement and then to update the member data.

```
cout << " Module " << module_id << "    Student "
   << student_id << endl ;
strcpy (student_identity, student_id) ;
strcpy (module_identity, module_id) ;
```

We copy the value from the parameter `student_id` into the member data area `student_identity` and the value from the parameter `module_id` into the member data area `module_identity` using the `strcpy` function. Recall that to use `strcpy`, we must include the header file `<string.h>`.

The remainder of the constructor calls member functions to acquire the marks and make the initial calculations as in previous versions of `initialise`.

Now by examining the revised program file, we can see how the parameters are used. First the declaration of the `geography_MK110` object.

```
student_marks_2Bb geography_MK110 ("MK110", "GEOG") ;
```

This specifies the string value **"MK110"** to be used as the first parameter of the constructor. As we have seen this will be transferred to the data member **student_identity** for the **geography_MK110** object. Similarly, the string value **"GEOG"** of the second parameter will be transferred to the data member **module_identity** of the same object.

The creation of the **maths_JP100** object has only one parameter.

```
student_marks_2Bb maths_JP100 ("JP100") ;
```

In this case **"JP100"** will be transferred to the data member **student_identity** for the **maths_JP100** object. The default parameter (**MATHS**) will be used for the second parameter and will be placed in **module_identity** for this object. Note that when default parameters are used, they must come at the end of the parameter list.

An example of the output when the program in **sum_2.cpp** is executed is given in figure 10.6.

```
Module GEOG    Student MK110
Enter examination mark no. 1 55
.  .  .
Enter examination mark no. 5 65
Enter first practical mark (or 999) 75
Enter next practical mark (or 999) 999

Student identity: MK110 for Module: GEOG
Exam mark is 63 Practical mark is 75
The sum of the marks is 138
 Module MATHS    Student JP100
Enter examination mark no. 1 63
.  .  .
Enter examination mark no. 5 41
Enter first practical mark (or 999) 74
Enter next practical mark (or 999) 999

Student identity: JP100 for Module: MATHS
Exam mark is 55 Practical mark is 74
The sum of the marks is 129
```

Figure 10.6

10.3 Destructors

As constructors reserve memory (and execute other initialisation operations), we have **destructors** to return memory to the memory management system. The **default destructor** is called automatically for an instance of an object when "it falls out of scope". What this means, in most cases, is that the memory is always returned when the function in which an object is created finishes; the object is no longer required.

Programmer-defined destructors are required when **dynamic objects** are used, this will be covered in chapter 14.

10.4 Exercises

10.4.1 Please refer to the examples in figures 10.1 and 10.2, then answer the following questions.

(a) What are the two main purposes of a constructor?

(b) How does a constructor prototype differ from a prototype of a member function?

(c) What is the effect of the following statement?

```
student_marks_2Ba geography_JP100 ;
```

10.4.2 Please refer to the examples in figures 10.4 and 10.5, then answer the following questions.

(a) How is a default parameter defined?

(b) What is the effect of the following statement?

```
student_marks_2Bb geography_MK110 ("MK110",
    "GEOG") ;
```

(c) What is the effect of the following statement?

```
student_marks_2Bb maths_JP100 ("JP100") ;
```

10.4.3 Make changes as necessary to the examples in figures 10.1 and 10.2 to achieve the following revised specification.

The data are entered as before and the sum and weighted average are displayed whenever a **student_marks_2Ba** object is created.

10.4.4 Produce a header file (**cube.h**) and a program file (**assig104.cpp**) to achieve the specification described by the model in figure 10.7 and the pseudo-code in figure 10.8 for the member functions and figure 10.9 for the main program.

A value for the member data should be obtained from a parameter of the constructor and both member functions should be called in the constructor.

The volume and area should be displayed, with appropriate text, to 2 decimal places.

Note, **<math.h>** includes a function **pow** to raise a value to a given power. The mathematical expression $y = x^n$ is written in C++ as

```
y = pow (x, n) ;
```

```
Class : cube

length of side (float)

Cube (constructor)
Display volume
Display surface area
```

Figure 10.7

```
cube::cube (length)
   Store length of side
   Call display_volume
   Call display_surface_area

cube::display_volume
   Declare volume variable
   Calculate volume (length³)
   Display volume

cube::display_surface_area
   Declare area variable
   Calculate surface area (length² * 6)
   Display surface area
```

Figure 10.8

```
main
   Declare die (5.5) of type cube
   Declare oxo (1.2) of type cube
```

Figure 10.9

11 Introduction to Arrays

Objectives for this chapter
Familiarity with the C++ programming terms and concepts:
- array declarations and bounds
- array indexes
- array initialisation.

Ability to:
- understand the need for arrays
- understand and write simple C++ programs that use one-dimensional arrays.

11.1 The need for arrays

In many computer programs we often have to deal with an ordered collection of related items of the same data type, which we need to store for later use in the program. In such cases we do not store each item in a separate variable, but rather as an ordered collection of storage areas identified by one name; we then refer to an individual area by this name and its position in the set. For example, the marks of all the students for a module could be regarded as an ordered collection of integers; if we needed to store this data in a computer program we could do so as an ordered collection of data items with one name, say **marks**.

11.2 Using an array

Let us consider a simple example. We have just twelve students, with student numbers 0 to 11. A student is awarded a merit for a module if the mark exceeds the average mark for that module. A program is required to read in the mark for each student and display, below a heading, the student number and mark of those who qualify for a merit. The original **student_marks** object class and all the derived classes used so far have been concerned with the performance of a single student in a single module. As we now have a module studied by twelve students, we introduce a new object class **module**. A simple model for this object class is given in as an object schema in figure 11.1.

There are two basic tasks to be accomplished, and for both of these we

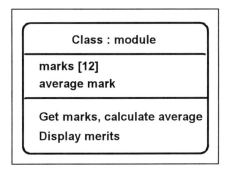

Figure 11.1

need to access all twelve marks.

    (i)   Find the average of the twelve marks.

    (ii) Compare each individual mark with the average and display the student number and mark of those that exceed the average.

We could enter the data twice, once for each task, but clearly this would be error-prone and time-consuming. We could store the data in a computer file and then access the file, but again this could be very time-consuming if we had a large amount of data. So we enter the data once in achieving task (i) and at the same time store the data in a block of storage (known as an **array**). Next, we access the array to achieve task (ii).

We can visualise the array, that is the data member **marks** **[12]**, as illustrated in figure 11.2.

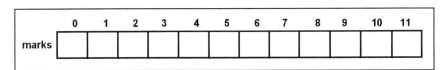

Figure 11.2

Notice that the array has one name but twelve store locations each capable of holding a mark. Each of the twelve individual store locations (which we call the **elements** of the array) is identified by means of its position or **index**. The first store location is for the element of **marks** with an index of **0**, the second store location is for the element of **marks** with an index of **1**, and so on. We can access any particular element of the array, use its value in an expression, and assign it a new value by referring to the name of the array together with the index of the element we wish to address.

Consider the following code

```
marks [3] = 67 ;
index = 7 ;
marks [index + 2] = marks [3] + 10 ;
```

this would result in

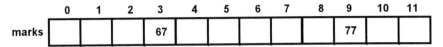

The most straightforward way of entering the data is to simply enter the marks in student number order, hence implying the student number (which is also the array index) by the order in which the mark is entered. The first mark entered would be for student with student number 0 and so on until all 12 marks have been entered. The pseudo-code for task (i) is given in figure 11.3 and for task (ii) in figure 11.4.

```
module::get_marks
    Declare terminator variable
    Initialise total mark (=0)
    FOR student index goes from 0 to 11 in steps of 1
        Prompt for and accept mark into array element
            indexed by student index
        Add mark to total mark
    Skip over final newline character
    Compute average mark
```

Figure 11.3

```
module::display_merits
    Display headings
    FOR student index goes from 0 to 11 in steps of 1
        IF mark in array element indexed by student
            index > average
        Display student index as student number
        Display mark in array element indexed by
            student index
```

Figure 11.4

The C++ code for the above is given in figure 11.5 as the header file (**module.h**) containing the object class **module**. A simple program file (**average.cpp**) creating an object and using these functions is given in figure 11.6.

The object class definition in figure 11.5 contains two items of member data. The first is the declaration of an array of integers to be used for storing the marks:

```
int marks [no_of_marks] ;
```

Arrays are declared by specifying the type of values to be stored (**int**) followed

```
// MODULE.H
// The object class module
#include <iostream.h>
    const int no_of_marks = 12 ;
class module
    {
    public :
        void get_marks () ;
        void display_merits () ;
    protected :
        int marks [no_of_marks] ;
        int average_mark ;
    } ;

void module::get_marks ()
    {
    char terminator ;
    int total = 0 ;
    for (int student_index = 0 ; student_index <
        no_of_marks ; ++ student_index)
        {
        cout << "Enter a mark for student no. "
            << student_index << " : " ;
        cin >> marks [student_index] ;
        total += marks [student_index] ;
        }
    cin.get (terminator) ;
    average_mark = total / no_of_marks ;
    }

void module::display_merits ()
    {
    cout << endl << "Students with merits" << endl ;
    for (int student_index = 0 ; student_index <
        no_of_marks ; ++ student_index)
        {
        if (marks [student_index] > average_mark)
            cout << "No. " << student_index << "   "
                << marks [student_index] << endl ;
        }
    }
```

Figure 11.5

```
// AVERAGE.CPP
// A program to get marks for 12 students and display
// those that are above the average
#include "module.h"
void main ()
    {
    module computing ;
    computing.get_marks () ;
    computing.display_merits () ;
    }
```

Figure 11.6

by an identifier by which we will refer to all elements of the array (**marks**) and the number of elements in the array (12, the value from the constant **no_of_marks**) in square brackets. As the index of array elements always starts at 0 in C++, this latter component also specifies the range of the indexes: 0 to 11.

Note that the constant **no_of_marks** is declared outside the class declaration and can be used within the whole of the header file and any program that includes it. We choose to use a constant here because we will refer to the maximum number of elements of the array a number of times (in the **for** loops and the calculation of the average). If we need to change the number of elements in a future revision of the program, we need only make one change to the constant value rather than searching for all occurrences of it.

The function **get_marks** uses a **for** loop to store the entries from the keyboard in the array and to compute the total of these marks.

```
for (int student_index = 0 ; student_index <
    no_of_marks ; ++ student_index)
    {
    cout << "Enter a mark for student no. "
       << student_index << " : " ;
    cin >> marks [student_index] ;
    total += marks [student_index] ;
    }
```

The **for** statement declares the variable **student_index** and uses it as a counter to control the number of iterations of the loop. In the first repeated statement, **student_index** is used in the prompt as the student number to identify the mark to be entered. Next, **cin** is used to accept an integer from the input stream into an element of the array **marks**. The element is indexed by **student_index**, hence when the prompt asks for a mark for student no. 4, the mark accepted from the input stream will be placed into the element of the array with index = 4, that is the fifth element. Finally, the marks total (**total**) is increased by the same value using the same syntax to identify the mark: array identifier (marks) followed by the index to the required element (student_index) in square brackets.

The display_merits member function uses a similar for loop to access each element of the array in turn. Within the body of the loop an individual element is accessed twice using marks [student_index].

The method of entering the data in the above example is somewhat restrictive. We could use a more flexible way by entering both the student number and the mark for a student. In this case the data would not need to be in student number order and it would not need to be complete, in that any mark not entered for a student could be assumed to be zero. This would, of course, necessitate initialising all elements of the array to zero before obtaining any marks. The pseudo-code for this approach is given in figure 11.7 and the C++ header file (module1.h) is given in figure 11.8.

```
module1::get_marks
    Declare variables
    Initialise total mark (=0)
    Initialise all array elements (=0)
    Prompt for and accept 1st student number and mark
    WHILE student number not 999
        Store mark in array element indexed by student
            number
        Add mark to total mark
        Prompt for and accept next student number and
            mark
    Skip over final newline character
    Compute average mark
```

Figure 11.7

Here we have inherited the class module but over-ridden the member function get_marks. Notice first the technique for initialising all elements of the array.

```
for (int index = 0 ; index < no_of_marks ;
    ++ index)
    marks [index] = 0 ;
```

We use a for loop that declares the variable index with an initial value of zero. Each time round the loop an element of the marks array is set to zero starting at the element with an index of zero through to the element with an index of 11.

For the main loop, the while, we use a read-ahead technique because we do not know at the outset how many times we are going to go round the loop. As mentioned in chapter 5, when cin is used to obtain an integer value it will first ignore any spaces and newline characters. So the student number and mark

```
// MODULE1.H
// The object class module_1
#include "module.h"
class module_1 : public module
    {
    public :
        void get_marks () ;
    } ;

void module_1::get_marks ()
    {
    char terminator ;
    int student_number,
        mark ;
    int total = 0 ;
    for (int index = 0 ; index < no_of_marks ;
        ++ index)
        marks [index] = 0 ;
    cout << "Enter student no. and mark: " ;
    cin >> student_number >> mark ;
    while (student_number != 999)
        {
        marks [student_number] = mark ;
        total += mark ;
        cout << "Enter student no. and mark: " ;
        cin >> student_number >> mark ;
        }
    cin.get (terminator) ;
    average_mark = total / no_of_marks ;
    }
```

Figure 11.8

can be typed with any number of spaces between them. Within the body of the loop we process the current student number and mark then get the next student number and mark (the student number may be the end-marker 999).

```
marks [student_number] = mark ;
total += mark ;
cout << "Enter student no. and mark: " ;
cin >> student_number >> mark ;
```

We use the value obtained in **student_number** as an index in assigning the value obtained in **mark** to the corresponding element of the array **marks**. Note that in this simplified program we do not check that **student_number** is a valid index, that is, in the range 0 to 11. If a user typed an invalid student number, unpredictable results or a run-time error would occur because the first line in the above code would attempt to assign mark to an element that does not exist.

11.3 Exercises

11.3.1 Please refer to the example in figure 11.5, and answer the following questions.
   (a) What is the basic reason for using an array in this example?
   (b) What three things need to be written to declare an array?
   (c) What two things need to be written to access an element of an array?
   (d) Why is the **for** loop construct used here?
   (e) What are the allowable index values for the array **marks**?
   (f) If the students were now numbered from 1 to 12, what changes would you make to **get_marks** and **display_merits**? Hint: for each function, you only need to change the **cout** statement within the **for** loop.

11.3.2 Please refer to the example in figure 11.8, and answer the following questions.
   (a) Why is it necessary to initialise all elements of the array to zero?
   (b) Why is a **while** loop used in **get_marks**?
   (c) What would happen if a student number of 13, say, was entered?
   (d) What changes would have to be made to calculate the average of the marks actually entered at the keyboard?
   (e) What two advantages does this approach for reading values into an array have over the one used in figure 11.5?

11.3.3 Make changes to the example in figure 11.5 to achieve the following revised specification.
   (a) The number of marks is now 18.
   (b) A merit is awarded for the highest mark in the group. This could be awarded to more than one student so it is necessary to establish the highest mark in **get_marks** and then use this in **display_merits**.

11.3.4 Make changes to the example in figure 11.8 to prevent the use of an incorrect index. This can be achieved by repeatedly asking the user to enter a student number and mark until a student number in the correct range is entered (see, for example, figure 9.6). You should define a new function **get_a_mark** with the formal parameters **student_no** and **a_mark** and replace the **cout** statement followed by the **cin** in **get_marks** by a call to this new function.

11.3.5   Produce a header file (**sales.h**) and a program file
(**assig115.cpp**) to achieve the following specification.

A program is required to accept 20 sales figures (as real numbers) in
order of sales person's reference number (in the range 10 to 29
inclusive). Then the reference number of each sales person who
achieved sales of at least 80% of the best sales figure is displayed. At
the end, the number of sales persons who have achieved this figure is
displayed.

A sample screen dialogue is shown in figure 11.9. The model for the
object class **sales** is given in figure 11.10 and the pseudo-code for
the member functions is in figure 11.11.

```
Enter sales figure for sales person 10: 10.4
Enter sales figure for sales person 11: 30.1
Enter sales figure for sales person 12: 100.2
Enter sales figure for sales person 13: 80.7
Enter sales figure for sales person 14: 50.4
.  .  .
Enter sales figure for sales person 29: 18.9
Sales person 12 achieved target
Sales person 13 achieved target
Sales person 18 achieved target
3 sales persons achieved target
```

Figure 11.9

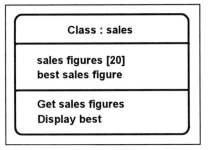

Figure 11.10

```
sales::get_sales
   Declare terminator variable
   Initialise best sales figure (= 0)
   FOR sales index from 0 to 19 in steps of 1
      Prompt for sales figure (sales index + 10)
      Accept sales figure into array
      IF sales figure exceeds best sales figure
         Store sales figure as best sales figure
   Skip over final newline character

sales::display_best
   Declare and initialise count (= 0)
   FOR sales index goes from 0 to 19 in steps of 1
      IF sales figure in array (indexed by sales
         index) exceeds 80% of best sales figure
         Display reference number (sales index + 10)
         Increase count by 1
   Display count
```

Figure 11.11

12 Arrays of Objects

Objectives for this chapter
Familiarity with the C++ programming terms and concepts:
- arrays of objects
- aggregation.

Ability to:
- understand and write simple C++ programs that use arrays of objects
- distinguish between object aggregation (composition) and inheritance (classification).

12.1 Using an array of objects

Consider a slight variation to the problem described in section 11.2 of the previous chapter. Suppose that we now want to obtain the twelve exam marks for a module and display the exam mark and the student identity (as opposed to student number) of those students whose exam mark is above the average.

In the previous chapter, we read in the mark for each student and store the marks in an array, **int marks [no_of_marks]**, within the object class **module**. As an alternative, we note that the **student_marks** object classes already have member data for a student (for example, **exam_mark**, and **student_identity**). So we could make use of this by defining a new object class for a module (**module_A**) that has as one of its data members an array of **student_marks** objects.

In the solution to this problem, we will use the derived object class **student_marks_2Bc** that contains two extra necessary functions. The header file for this, **marks2bc.h**, is given in figure 12.1.

The two public member functions simply return the values of member data, **exam_mark** and **student_identity**. They are necessary because these data items are described as **protected** in their original definition, which means that they can only be accessed by objects of the class in which they are declared or any derived classes, and we need to access them in the object class **module_A**.

The second function, **return_student_identity**, has a result type of **char*** which is formally a pointer to an item of type **char**. We will discuss

```
// MARKS2BC.H
// The object class student_marks_2Bc
#include "marks2b.h"
class student_marks_2Bc : public student_marks_2B
    {
    public :
        int return_exam_mark () ;
        char* return_student_identity () ;
    } ;

int student_marks_2Bc::return_exam_mark ()
    {
    return exam_mark ;
    }

char* student_marks_2Bc::return_student_identity ()
    {
    return student_identity ;
    }
```

Figure 12.1

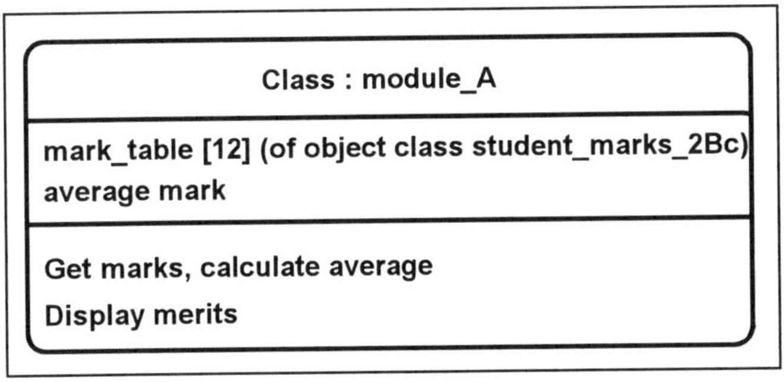

Figure 12.2

pointers later. For the moment, please accept that it is the way in which we are able to return a string as the result of a function.

The model for **module_A** is given in figure 12.2 and the C++ class definition from **module_a.h** in figure 12.3.

In the previous chapter, we declared an array as

```
int marks [no_of_marks] ;
```

and noted that each element of the array holds a value of the integer type **int**. Similarly, when using the declaration for an array of objects, the format is the

```
// MODULE_A.H
// The object class module_A
#include "marks2bc.h"
   const int no_of_marks = 12 ;
class module_A
   {
   protected :
      int average_mark ;
      student_marks_2Bc mark_table [no_of_marks] ;
   public :
      void get_marks () ;
      void display_merits () ;
   } ;
```

Figure 12.3

same. The type of the elements is given first (the object class
student_marks_2Bc), followed by the array identifier (mark_table) and
the array size (the constant no_of_marks):

```
   student_marks_2Bc mark_table [no_of_marks] ;
```

Each element of the array holds a value of the object class
student_marks_2Bc; in other words each element of mark_table is an
instance of this object class. Hence when an instance of the object class
module_A is created, this in turn creates the 12 instances of
student_marks_2Bc that make up this array.

The array is initialised in the function get_marks (shown as figure
12.4) and used in the function display_merits (in figure 12.5).

```
void module_A::get_marks ()
   {
   int total = 0 ;
   for (int student_index = 0 ; student_index <
      no_of_marks ; ++ student_index)
      {
      mark_table [student_index].initialise () ;
      total += mark_table
         [student_index].return_exam_mark () ;
      }
   average_mark = total / no_of_marks ;
   }
```

Figure 12.4

```
void module_A::display_merits ()
   {
   cout << endl << "Students with merits" << endl ;
   for (int student_index = 0 ; student_index <
      no_of_marks ; ++ student_index)
      {
      int mark = mark_table
         [student_index].return_exam_mark () ;
      if (mark > average_mark)
         cout << "Identity " << mark_table
            [student_index].return_student_identity ()
            << "   " << mark << endl ;
      }
   }
```

Figure 12.5

We initialise each element of the array, a **student_marks_2Bc** object, and accumulate the total exam mark in the function **get_marks**. Note that in the body of the loop there is a function call to the inherited **initialise** function as well as an assignment statement to accumulate the total.

```
mark_table [student_index].initialise () ;
total += mark_table
   [student_index].return_exam_mark () ;
```

We call the **initialise** function for each of the objects in the array using the index in **student_index**. Notice the format here. First, as usual, we have the array identifier followed by the index in square brackets. Then we have a the member access operator followed by the required member of the object class, that is the function **initialise**. Next, in the assignment statement, we add to the local variable **total** the result of calling the **return_exam_mark** function for the object with the same index.

We use similar code in the member function **display_merits**.

```
int mark = mark_table
   [student_index].return_exam_mark () ;
if (mark > average_mark)
   cout << "Identity " << mark_table
      [student_index].return_student_identity ()
      << "   " << mark << endl ;
```

For each object in the array, we call the **return_exam_mark** function using the index **student_index**. This statement and the extra variable (**mark**) are not strictly necessary. They have been used to optimise the code, we use **mark** instead of calling the function twice: once in the relational expression of the **if** and again in the `cout`.

In the `cout` statement, we output the student identity of the currently indexed object by calling the function `return_student_identity`.

Figure 12.6 is an example of a program file (`merits.cpp`) that uses the object class `module_A`.

```
// MERITS.CPP
// A program to get exam marks for 12 students
// and display those that are above average
#include "module_a.h"
void main ()
   {
   module_A computing ;
   computing.get_marks () ;
   computing.display_merits () ;
   }
```

Figure 12.6

Figure 12.7 is an abbreviated example of the dialogue that is seen on the monitor screen when the program is run. As soon as the object `computing` is created, memory is allocated for the array `mark_table`. Because the array is an array of objects, this in turn creates the 12 instances of `student_marks_2Bc` that make up this array.

When `get_marks` is called, each element of the array is initialised by calling the `initialise` function of the object class `student_marks_2Bc` that was inherited from `student_marks_2B`. This causes the interactive acquisition of the student and module identities and exam and practical marks represented in figure 12.7. The last five lines are produced as a result of the call to `display_merits`.

12.2 Aggregation

This technique of using object classes in the definition of another object class is an example of partial **aggregation** or **composition**. It is quite different from inheritance where we have seen derived classes created from base classes. We can distinguish the two by considering some examples. In chapter 2 we briefly described an inheritance or **classification hierarchy** of a base class **employee** from which were derived the derived classes **manager**, **technician** and **secretary**. We say here that a manager or technician is 'a kind of' employee'. On the other hand, if we had an object class for say, a department, it could comprise a manager object and a secretary object as well as other items. In this case we say that the object class **department** is an aggregate or composition of a **manager** object, a **secretary** object and so on.

```
Enter student identity code MK100
Enter module identity code COMP
Enter examination mark no. 1 20
. . .
Enter examination mark no. 5 14
Enter first practical mark (or 999) 999
Enter student identity code JG120
. . .
Enter examination mark no. 5 12
Enter first practical mark (or 999) 999
. . .

. . .
Enter student identity code JG200
. . .
Enter examination mark no. 5 18
Enter first practical mark (or 999) 999

Students with merits
Identity MK100   67
Identity SA140   68
Identity JG200   69
```

Figure 12.7

In the above example (see figure 12.2), the object class
student_marks_2Bc is a derived class of **student_marks_2B** (an
example of inheritance) and the object class **module_A** contains an array of
objects of type **student_marks_2Bc** (an example of aggregation).

12.3 Exercises

12.3.1 Please refer to the example in figure 12.1, and answer the following
questions.
   (a) Why are the two member functions of **student_marks_2Bc**
      necessary?
   (b) What are the result types for the two member functions?
   (c) Which inherited function is used to obtain values for the inherited
      data members? From which object class is it inherited?

12.3.2 Please refer to the example in figures 12.3 to 12.5, and answer the
following questions.
   (a) Describe the three components of the array declaration in the
      object class definition.

(b) How many times is the function `initialise` called in
`get_marks`? Describe what happens each time it is called (see figure 8.3).

(c) Describe the coding optimisation used in `display_merits`.
What are the advantages and disadvantages of its use?

(d) Give an example of inheritance and an example of partial aggregation.

12.3.3   Produce two header files (`person.h` and `members.h`) and a program file (`assig123.cpp`) to achieve the following specification.

The header file `person.h` has a simple object class definition as indicated by the model given in figure 12.8 and the pseudo-code in figure 12.9 to allow an object to be initialised with a person's surname (a maximum of 14 characters) and display the surname.

A program is required to accept 10 surnames and then to display them in the reverse order. The model for the object class `members` is given in figure 12.10 and the pseudo-code for the member functions is in figure 12.11.

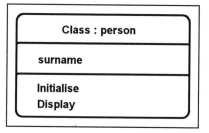

```
Class : person

surname

Initialise
Display
```

Figure 12.8

```
person::display
    display surname

person::initialise
    Declare terminator variable
    Prompt for and accept surname
    Skip over terminating character
```

Figure 12.9

```
┌─────────────────────────────────────────┐
│  ┌───────────────────────────────────┐  │
│  │         Class : members           │  │
│  ├───────────────────────────────────┤  │
│  │ person list [10] (of object class person) │
│  ├───────────────────────────────────┤  │
│  │ Get names                         │  │
│  │ Display names (in reverse order)  │  │
│  └───────────────────────────────────┘  │
└─────────────────────────────────────────┘
```

Figure 12.10

```
members::get_names
    FOR person index goes from 0 to 9 in steps of 1
        Call initialise for object person list
            indexed by person index

members::display_names
    Display heading "Membership in reverse order"
    FOR person index goes from 9 down to 0 in steps
        of 1
        Call display for object person list indexed
            by person index
```

Figure 12.11

13 Two-dimensional Arrays

<hr>

Objectives for this chapter
Familiarity with the C++ programming terms and concepts:
- two-dimensional arrays
- the manipulator `setw`
- shorthand technique for initialising an array.

Ability to:
- understand and write simple C++ programs that use two-dimensional arrays.

<hr>

13.1 Using a two-dimensional array

One-dimensional arrays are arrays whose components are single data items (single numbers, characters and so on). An array whose elements are themselves one-dimensional arrays is called a two-dimensional array. Likewise we can define three-dimensional arrays and so on. Let us now consider an example that processes a two-dimensional array.

Consider a table of student marks for a small course. Say we have six students studying four modules as illustrated in figure 13.1.

		student index					
		0	**1**	**2**	**3**	**4**	**5**
module index	**0**	15	5	50	60	44	55
	1	25	35	50	51	60	55
	2	75	100	25	25	65	73
	3	50	45	35	80	76	95

Figure 13.1

We could store the marks in a one-dimensional array of 24 elements, but this is not very convenient if we want to access all the marks of a single student or all the marks for one module. Just as places on a map need to be defined by two co-ordinates, we find that a two-dimensional array allows us to access any element by reference to two indexes. In our example, we can access any mark as long as we know the index that tells us which module is required (module index) and the index that tells us which student is required (student index).

We declare a two-dimensional array as follows.

```
const int no_of_modules = 4 ;
const int no_of_students = 6 ;
. . .
int marks [no_of_modules] [no_of_students] ;
```

We can now think of a two-dimensional array as having rows and columns. In figure 13.1, we can visualise an array where we have one row for each module and one column for each student. Notice that the order of the constants in the array declaration is important. The first one gives the number of rows (4) and the second gives the number of columns (6). Then, to access an array element, the first index will indicate the row and the second the column. Thus, **marks [2] [4]** refers to the mark from row 3 (module index 2) and column 5 (student index 4) that has the value 65 in our example in figure 13.1. Similarly, it can be seen that **marks [1] [3]** contains the value 51 and **marks [2] [0]** has the value 75.

Let us now consider a problem that uses the above two-dimensional array to store and access marks. We will produce a program to accept the marks from the keyboard, then display the marks on the screen in the form of a table with one row for each module and the module's average mark at the end of each row. The output is given in figure 13.2, from which we can see that for each row we must first output the module number, then the mark for each student, and finally the average mark for the module.

	0	1	2	3	4	5	Average
Module No. 0	15	5	50	60	44	55	38
Module No. 1	25	35	50	51	60	55	46
Module No. 2	75	100	25	25	65	73	60
Module No. 3	50	45	35	80	76	95	63

Figure 13.2

As when using a one-dimensional array, we have two tasks.
  (i) Store the marks in the array.
  (ii) Process the array to display the table.

Also, we can accept all 24 marks in a set order or enter the module number and student number for each mark. We will describe both approaches. First, the straightforward approach of entering all 24 marks module by module, that is all six marks for module 0, followed by all six marks for module 1 and so on. A model for a course with the necessary array as a data member and the required functions is shown in figure 13.3. The pseudo-code for task (i), **get_marks**, is given in figure 13.4 and for task (ii), **display_marks**, in figure 13.5.

```
Class : course

marks [4] [6]

Get marks
Display marks as a table
```

Figure 13.3

```
course::get_marks
    Declare terminator variable
    FOR module index goes from 0 to 3 in steps of 1
        FOR student index goes from 0 to 5 in steps
            of 1
        Prompt for mark
        Accept mark into array element indexed by
            module index and student index
    Skip over final newline character
```

Figure 13.4

```
course::display_marks
    Declare variable module total
    Display column headings
    FOR module index goes from 0 to 3 in steps of 1
        Initialise mark total for a module (=0)
        Display row title
        FOR student index goes from 0 to 5 in steps
            of 1
        Display mark indexed by module index and
            student index
        Accumulate mark total for a module
    Compute and display average mark for a module
```

Figure 13.5

The structure of the nested for loops in **get_marks** (figure 13.4) reflects the order in which the marks are to be entered. Starting with a module index of 0, the student index goes from 0 to 5; this is repeated for a module index of 1 then 2 then 3. Similarly, in **display_marks** (figure 13.5) the process of dealing with a module, that is producing a row of the output, is repeated for a module index of 0 then 1 then 2 then 3.

The C++ code for the above is given in figures 13.6 to 13.8. The class definition of **course** from the header file (**course.h**) is given in figure 13.6, the two member functions are shown separately in figures 13.7 and 13.8.

```cpp
// COURSE.H
// The object class course
#include <iostream.h>
#include <iomanip.h>
   const int no_of_modules = 4 ;
   const int no_of_students = 6 ;
class course
   {
   public :
      void get_marks () ;
      void display_marks () ;
   protected :
      int marks [no_of_modules] [no_of_students] ;
   } ;
```

Figure 13.6

```cpp
void course::get_marks ()
   {
   char terminator ;
   for (int module_index = 0 ; module_index <
      no_of_modules ; ++ module_index)
      {
      for (int student_index = 0 ; student_index <
         no_of_students ; ++ student_index)
         {
         cout << "Enter a mark for module no: "
            << module_index << " student no: "
            << student_index << " : " ;
         cin >> marks [module_index]
            [student_index] ;
         }
      }
   cin.get (terminator) ;
   }
```

Figure 13.7

```
void course::display_marks ()
  {
  int module_total ;
  cout <<
          "           0   1   2   3   4   5 "
    << "Average" << endl ;
  for (int module_index = 0 ; module_index <
     no_of_modules ; ++ module_index)
     {
     module_total = 0 ;
     cout << "Module No. " << module_index
        << "    " ;
     for (int student_index = 0 ; student_index <
        no_of_students ; ++ student_index)
        {
        cout << setw (4) << marks [module_index]
           [student_index] ;
        module_total += marks [module_index]
           [student_index] ;
        }
     cout << setw (5) << module_total /
        no_of_students << endl ;
     }
  }
```

Figure 13.8

The two-dimensional array is declared as a protected data member in the class definition of **course**.

int marks [no_of_modules] [no_of_students] ;

As we have seen for single-dimension arrays, we specify the type of values to be stored (**int**) followed by an identifier by which we will refer to all elements of the array (**marks**) and the number of elements in the array. For two-dimensional arrays we need two indexes, so we specify 4, the value from the constant **no_of_modules**, and 6, the value from the constant **no_of_students**.

The function **get_marks** uses two nested **for** loops to store the entries from the keyboard in the array. The outer loop changes the value of **module_index** from 0 to 3 in steps of 1. The inner loop changes the value of **student_index** from 0 to 5 in steps of 1 four times. The first time when **module_index** is 0, then when it is 1, then 2, then 3. Hence the body of the inner loop is executed 24 times.

Note the statements that make up the body of the inner loop.

```
cout << "Enter a mark for module no: "
    << module_index << " student no: "
    << student_index << " : " ;
cin >> marks [module_index] [student_index] ;
```

The prompt uses both of the loop counters **module_index** and **student_index** to identify the mark to be entered. Next, **cin** is used to accept an integer from the input stream into an element of the array **marks**. The element of the array is indexed by the two counters **module_index** and **student_index**, hence when the prompt asks for a mark for module no. 0 student no. 4, the mark accepted from the input stream will be placed into the element of the array with **module_index** = 0 and **student_index** = 4.

The **display_marks** member function uses similar nested **for** loops to access each element of the array in turn starting at the first one in module 0, that is the one with a module index of 0 and a student index of 0. Notice that for each module (0 to 3), the module total is set to zero, the row title is produced, then the inner **for** loop processes all of the student marks for the module, then the average mark for the module is computed and displayed. The processing of the inner for loop displays the appropriate mark and accumulates the module total.

```
cout << setw (4) << marks [module_index]
    [student_index] ;
module_total += marks [module_index]
    [student_index] ;
```

In the above, first notice a new feature. The manipulator **setw** is used to set the field width (4 in this case) of the following output. The effect is that when a mark is displayed, it will be right-justified in four character positions, for example, a mark of 5 has three spaces output before the digit 5, a mark of 35 will be preceded by two spaces. This ensures that the marks are tabulated below each other, irrespective of the number of digits involved, as illustrated by the second column in the table in figure 13.2. The manipulator is defined in the header file **iomanip.h** which we have already referred to. We use it also in the final **cout** statement of the function for the average mark.

As we can infer from the above, the identifier **marks** must always be used in conjunction with two indexes. The first must always have a value in the range 0 to 3 and the second in the range 0 to 5. Failure to ensure that the indexes are within the correct ranges will cause the program to give unpredictable results or cause a run-time error. In this program, we are safe in that the values of the indexes are generated by the **for** statements. However, if we mistakenly used **student_index** as the first index and **module_index** as the second, we would have an index value greater than 3 for the first index; this would cause the problems we have indicated.

13.2 An alternative approach for entering the data

The alternative approach to obtaining the data for the array is by accepting the module number and student number with each mark, with the consequent advantage that the marks do not need to be entered in any specific order; we can use the default value of zero for any mark not entered by initialising the array so that all elements are zero initially. The pseudo-code for a revised `get_marks` function is given in figure 13.9 and the C++ code in figure 13.10.

```
course::get_marks (revised version)
   Declare variables
   Initialise all array elements (=0)
   Prompt for and accept first module number,
      student number and mark
   WHILE module number not = 999
      Store mark in array element indexed by module
         number and student number
      Prompt for and accept next module number,
         student number and mark
   Skip over final newline character
```

Figure 13.9

To initialise all elements of the two-dimensional array we have:

```
for (int module_counter = 0 ; module_counter <
   no_of_modules ; ++ module_counter)
   for (int student_counter = 0 ;
      student_counter < no_of_marks ;
      ++ student_counter)
      marks [module_counter] [student_counter]
         = 0 ;
```

Here, we have used nested **for** loops that declare counters with an initial value of zero. Each time through the inner loop an element of the **marks** array is set to zero starting at the element with a module index of zero and student index of zero through to the element with a module index of 3 and a student index of 5. It is necessary to use this technique when initialising an array that is a member of an object class. However, there is a shorthand technique available for locally declared arrays. For example, we can declare a one-dimensional array with all elements initialised to zero by:

```
int totals [no_of_totals] = {0} ;
```

Or, for a two-dimensional array with all elements zero, we can use:

```
float results [no_of_rows] [no_of_columns] = {0} ;
```

For the main **while** loop, we again use a read-ahead technique. In the body of this loop we process the current module number, student number and

```
void course::get_marks ()
   {
   char terminator ;
   int module_number,
       student_number,
       mark ;
   for (int module_counter = 0 ; module_counter <
      no_of_modules ; ++ module_counter)
      for (int student_counter = 0 ;
          student_counter < no_of_marks ;
          ++ student_counter)
          marks [module_counter] [student_counter]
             = 0 ;
   cout <<
      "Enter module no. student no. then mark: " ;
   cin >> module_number >> student_number >> mark ;
   while (module_number != 999)
      {
      marks [module_number] [student_number]
         = mark ;
      cout <<
         "Enter module no. student no. then mark: " ;
      cin >> module_number >> student_number
         >> mark ;
      }
   cin.get (terminator) ;
   }
```

Figure 13.10

mark then get the next three values (the student number may be the end-marker
999).

```
marks [module_number] [student_number] = mark ;
cout
   << "Enter module no. student no. then mark: " ;
cin >> module_number >> student_number >> mark ;
```

We use the values obtained in **module_number** and **student_number** as
indexes in assigning the value obtained in **mark** to an element of the array
marks. Once more, we note that in this simplified program we do not check
that **module_number** or **student_number** has a valid index, that is, in
the ranges 0 to 3 and 0 to 5 respectively.

Finally, a simple program file (**table.cpp**) to create and use an object
of type **course** is provided in figure 13.11.

```
// TABLE.CPP
// A program to get 6 marks for each of 4 modules
// and display as a table with row averages
#include "course.h"
void main ()
    {
    course diploma ;
    diploma.get_marks () ;
    diploma.display_marks () ;
    }
```

Figure 13.11

13.3 Exercises

13.3.1   Please refer to the example in figures 13.6 to 13.8, and answer the following questions.

(a) Why do we use a two-dimensional array rather than a one-dimensional array here?

(b) Draw up a table under the headings **module_index** and **student_index** to illustrate the order in which these values change when used in the **cout** (and **cin**) statements in **get_marks**.

(c) What is the purpose of **setw** in **display_marks**?

(d) What might occur if we mistakenly used **student_index** as the first index and **module_index** as the second index when accessing the array **marks**?

13.3.2   Please refer to the example in figure 13.10, and answer the following questions.

(a) Why do we use **for** loops to initialise the two-dimensional array and why are they nested?

(b) In this initialisation, what would be the effect of swapping the **for** statements around, that is the inner one becomes the outer one and vice versa?

13.3.3   Make changes to the example in figure 13.8 to achieve the following revised specification.

The average mark is to be computed for each student and displayed as the last row, that is at the foot of the appropriate column. Note that you will need to use a one-dimensional array to hold the column (student) totals; this will have to be initialised to all zeros.

13.3.4 Produce a header file (**animals.h**) and a program file (**assig134.cpp**) to achieve the following specification.

A program is required to accept the age and weight, both integers, for a number of animals from the keyboard. There are twenty valid weights, namely the values between 20 and 39 inclusive, and ten valid ages, namely the values between 5 and 14 inclusive. The program displays a table on the monitor screen, as shown in figure 13.12, giving the number of animals with each possible combination of weight and age.

The model is given in figure 13.13 and the pseudo-code for two functions and a constructor is given in figure 13.14. The function **get_age_and_weight** has two parameters; you should use different identifiers for the actual and formal parameters. The program file should include the objects **cats** and **dogs** as instances of the class animals.

	5yrs	6yrs	7yrs	8yrs	...	14yrs
20kgs	7	7	5	4		0
21kgs	5	6	5	7		0
22kgs	4	6	8	8		0
23kgs	2	5	8	9		0
24kgs	2	4	6	9		1
...	...	...	...	...	...	...
39kgs	0	0	0	0	...	15

Figure 13.12

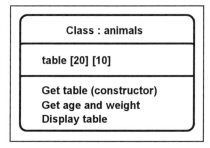

Figure 13.13

```
animals::animals
   Declare variables
   Initialise all array elements (=0)
   Call get_age_and_weight (age, weight)
   WHILE not end of the weights (age != 999)
      Add 1 to table element indexed by (weight -
         20) and (age - 5)
      Call get_age_and_weight (age, weight)
   Skip over final newline character

animals::get_age_and_weight (the_age, the_weight)
   DO
      Prompt for and accept age and weight
   WHILE not a valid age and weight

animals::display_table
   Display column headings
   FOR weight index goes from 0 to 19 in steps of 1
      Display row title
      FOR age index goes from 0 to 9 in steps of 1
         Display table indexed by weight index and
            age index
      Move cursor to next line
```

Figure 13.14

14 Object Lifetime and Dynamic Objects

Objectives for this chapter
Familiarity with the C++ programming terms and concepts:
- lifetime and scope
- the keyword `static`
- local variables and objects
- global variables and objects
- dynamic variables and objects
- memory allocation and addresses
- pointers and indirection
- **NULL** pointer value
- the function `malloc`
- arrow (`->`) and indirection (`*`) operators
- `new` and `delete` operators
- programmer-defined destructors.

Ability to:
- understand and write simple C++ programs that use dynamic objects.

14.1 Object lifetime

Some variables, including objects, exist for the complete duration of a program's execution; others may exist for only part of the time that the program is running, for example, just while a single function is being executed. As we shall see in the next chapter, we may wish to preserve the state of an object between different runs of a program or use an object in different programs.

The lifetime (period of existence) of any variable within a program, including an object, may be determined automatically by the compiler using what are called **scope** rules; alternatively it can be defined by the programmer using features of the C++ language. We will first illustrate the basic concepts using variables of type `int`.

14.2 The scope of variables

Consider the function **display_marks**, based on an example from chapter 13, given in figure 14.1.

```
// SCOPE1.H
   . . .
   const int no_of_modules = 4 ;
   const int no_of_students = 6 ;
class course
   {
   public :
      void display_marks () ;
   . . .
   protected :
      int marks [no_of_modules] [no_of_students] ;
   } ;

void course::display_marks ()
   {
   int module_total ;
   for (int module_index = 0 ; module_index <
      no_of_modules ; ++ module_index)
      {
      module_total = 0 ;
      for (int student_index = 0 ; student_index <
         no_of_students ; ++ student_index)
         {
         module_total += marks [module_index]
            [student_index] ;
         }
      cout << setw (5) << module_total << endl ;
      }
   cout << "All module totals displayed" ;
   }
```

Figure 14.1

The scope of a variable is that section of code in which the variable can be used. The compiler uses the position of a variable declaration to define, automatically, the scope of that variable. The variable **module_total** is declared at the start of the function **display_marks**. This means that when **display_marks** is called, memory is made available to it of the appropriate size for an **int**. Then when **display_marks** has finished, the memory is released back to the system; **module_total** in effect no longer exists. We say that the **scope** of `module_total` is within, or **local** to, the function `display_marks`.

The variable `student_index` is also local to the function `display_marks`, but its scope is more limited. A variable may only be used after it has been declared and within that part of the function enclosed by the braces immediately outside of its declaration; for `student_index` that is from line 8 of the function to the brace on line 15; for `module_total` that is the entire function.

The same rules apply to `const` identifiers. Since they are declared at the start of the header file, both the identifiers `no_of_modules` and `no_of_students` are **global** to the program (header) file; they may be used anywhere within the file or in any file, including the program file, that includes this header file. They are used in the function `display_marks` and in the declaration of the array `marks` in the object class definition.

The scope of the array `marks` is restricted by the C++ language (the keyword `protected`) so that the array may only be used within functions of the object class or any derived classes.

In all the above cases the declarations are automatic in the sense that the lifetime of the identifier is determined by the scope rules. If we want the value of a local variable in a function to be retained between calls to the function then we must declare the variable as **static**. For example, if for some reason we did not wish to lose the value of `module_total` after each call to `display_marks` was completed we would declare the variable as follows:

```
static int module_total ;
```

Now, if the first call resulted in a value of say 530 in `module_total`, when `display_marks` is called for a second time, `module_total` would start off with an initial value of 530.

This illustrates how the C++ keyword `static` can be used to extend the lifetime of a variable. Note that even though its value is retained, the variable `module_total` can still only be used within its normal scope, that is within `display_marks`.

14.3 The scope of objects

We can apply exactly the same lifetime and scope rules to objects. For example, consider the program file, given in figure 14.2, `scope2.cpp` that uses the `student_marks_2Ba` object class from `marks2ba.h`.

Here we have a global declaration for the object `history_MK350` which is then available throughout the program file. When the program is run, we say that the object is instantiated or created; memory is allocated and the initialisation specified within the programmer-written constructor is executed. The object's lifetime is the complete duration of the program's execution; it will

```
// SCOPE2.CPP
// A program to illustrate the scope of objects
#include "marks2ba.h"
    student_marks_2Ba history_MK350 ;
void main ()
    {
    for (int count = 1 ; count <= 3 ; ++ count)
        {
        student_marks_2Ba english_JP200 ;
        english_JP200.display_identities () ;
        english_JP200.display_marks () ;
        static student_marks_2Ba french_EP100 ;
        french_EP100.display_identities () ;
        french_EP100.display_marks () ;
        }
    history_MK350.display_identities () ;
    history_MK350.display_marks () ;
    }
```

Figure 14.2

exist from its creation until the program completes and is unloaded from the computer's memory.

The declaration of the object **english_JP200** is also automatic but it has local scope. An instance of the object class will be created and the constructor called each time round the **for** loop. Hence the member function calls that follow will be for a new object each time. Each time the body of the **for** loop completes the default destructor is used to release the memory assigned to the object.

The declaration of the object **french_EP100** is static and it has local scope. An instance of the object class will be created and the initialisation of the object's state within the constructor will be done just once, the first time round the **for** loop. The member function calls will use the same object each time round the loop. We say that the state of the object **french_EP100** persists, or that it retains its state.

Figure 14.3 illustrates the major operations when this program is executed. Note, in particular, that the data acquisition operations in the constructor occur once for each new object created, that is once for the global object **history_MK350**, once for the static local object **french_EP100** and three times for the automatic local object **english_JP100** each with a different value of counter.

Data acquisition (constructor called) for `history_MK350`
Data acquisition (constructor called) for `english_JP200`(counter = 1)
Display identities and marks for `english_JP200`
Data acquisition (constructor called) for `french_EP100`
Display identities and marks for `french_EP100`
Data acquisition (constructor called) for `english_JP200`(counter = 2)
Display identities and marks for `english_JP200`
Display identities and marks for `french_EP100`
Data acquisition (constructor called) for `english_JP200`(counter = 3)
Display identities and marks for `english_JP200`
Display identities and marks for `french_EP100`
Display identities and marks for `history_MK350`

Figure 14.3

14.4 Dynamic variables

In all our programs so far, we have been able to establish the need for each variable or object when the program is written and reserve appropriate memory by declaring an identifier. Sometimes, however, we do not know whether we need a variable or object until after the program has begun execution. For example, we may have a program that needs to store data about an unknown number of students. We could guess the maximum number and use array storage or we could use disk storage. In the former case this could lead to a large amount of redundant memory if the guess is too high, or the program having to be stopped if the guess is too low. In the latter case, the program would execute more slowly because it takes more time to write the data to a disk than to store it in memory.

The solution to this problem is to use **dynamic** data storage. Instead of reserving memory when an identifier is declared, a program is coded so that it obtains random access memory as the need arises during execution. The one draw-back to this is that we cannot use programmer chosen identifiers for such areas of memory; identifiers have meaning only within the source code not the executable object code. We overcome this problem by using a system of pointers to the locations or addresses of such areas of memory. Figure 14.4 is a demonstration C++ program that shows how an area of memory may be obtained and then used indirectly by using a pointer to its address.

There are a number of new programming features in this example. First we have the declaration of a pointer variable.

```
int* int_pointer = NULL ;
```

The asterisk after the type `int` indicates the declaration of a variable that is to

```cpp
// DYNAMIC.CPP
// Demonstrates the use of a simple dynamic
// variable
#include <stdlib.h>
#include <iostream.h>
void main ()
    {
    int* int_pointer = NULL ;
    int_pointer = (int*) malloc (sizeof (int)) ;
    if (int_pointer == NULL)
        {
        cout << "No memory available" << endl ;
        exit (1) ;
        }
    *int_pointer = 45 ;
    cout << "Address of memory used is "
        << int_pointer << endl ;
    cout << "Contents of memory used is "
        << *int_pointer << endl ;
    free (int_pointer) ;
    }
```

Figure 14.4

point to (or contain an address of) a memory area. Such variables are often called **pointer variables**. In this example, the identifier `int_pointer` has also been initialised. By convention, a pointer variable is not initialised to zero, but what is called a 'null value' is used; in C++ this is the constant **NULL**. While not necessary in this simple example, it is wise to consider the use of pointer variable initialisation.

The next statement looks somewhat complex. It is not necessary for you to understand it fully at this stage. It is one of the ways that memory can be allocated when a program is running.

```cpp
int_pointer = (int*) malloc (sizeof (int)) ;
```

The function **malloc** attempts to allocate memory and if successful gives the address (or pointer value) as the result of the function call; in this instance to be stored in `int_pointer`. The amount of memory to be allocated is given by the argument of **malloc**, computed here by using the operator **sizeof** to determine the amount necessary for an **int**. The cast **(int*)** is necessary to convert the result from **malloc** specifically to a pointer to an **int**.

Note that to use **malloc** we need to include the header file that references it, hence we have used **#include <stdlib.h>**.

Memory is not inexhaustible, so we need to ensure that memory has been correctly allocated. We do this by testing the pointer variable.

```
if (int_pointer == NULL)
    {
    cout << "No memory available" << endl ;
    exit (1) ;
    }
```

If **malloc** is unable to allocate sufficient memory, it returns a value of **NULL**. So, we simply test for this value. If we have been given a return value of **NULL**, we display a message then use the **exit** function found in the library **<stdlib.h>** to terminate the program. The argument 1 is a convention for abnormal program termination.

Next, we assign a value to the allocated memory area using the indirection operator * before the pointer variable.

```
*int_pointer = 45 ;
```

We say that 45 is assigned to the memory area pointed to by **int_pointer**, or the memory area at the address in **int_pointer**. This concept is illustrated by the next four lines of the program.

```
cout << "Address of memory used is "
    << int_pointer << endl ;
cout << "Contents of memory used is "
    << *int_pointer << endl ;
```

This gives the following output.

```
Address of memory used is 0x912d0004
Contents of memory used is 45
```

The first **cout** gives the contents of **int_pointer** which is a large strange-looking number that is one way of showing a memory address. The second **cout**, because it uses the indirection operator *, displays the contents of the memory whose address is stored in **int_pointer**.

Finally, we return the memory to the system.

```
free (int_pointer) ;
```

This is not strictly necessary in this program because memory is returned to the system automatically when a program terminates. However, we should always consider returning memory when it is no longer needed. The function **free**, found in **<stdlib.h>**, does this by taking as an argument a pointer variable containing a memory address.

14.5 Dynamic objects

Dynamic objects use the same principles as other dynamic variables. Let us consider an object class, that can have up to 10 **student_marks_2Ba** objects. A user may add a new object or remove the last object added, so the

```
┌─────────────────────────────────────────┐
│  ╭─────────────────────────────────────╮ │
│  │         Class : module_B            │ │
│  ├─────────────────────────────────────┤ │
│  │ student [10] (of pointers to        │ │
│  │ student_marks_2Ba)                  │ │
│  │ student index                       │ │
│  ├─────────────────────────────────────┤ │
│  │ Initialise index and array          │ │
│  │ (constructor)                       │ │
│  │ Get a student                       │ │
│  │ Remove a student                    │ │
│  │ Return memory (destructor)          │ │
│  ╰─────────────────────────────────────╯ │
└─────────────────────────────────────────┘
```

Figure 14.5

```
// MODULE_B.H
// The object class module_B
#include <stdlib.h>
#include "marks2Ba.h"
const int maximum_students = 10 ;
class module_B
    {
    protected :
       student_marks_2Ba* student [maximum_students] ;
       int student_index ;
    public :
       module_B () ;
       ~module_B () ;
       void get_student () ;
       void remove_student () ;
    } ;
```

Figure 14.6

number of objects being held at any one time will vary between 0 and 10. As a new object is added, the exam mark and practical mark are displayed. The model for the class (**module_B**) is given as figure 14.5 and the class definition is given in figure 14.6.

The first data member is an array of pointer variables

```
student_marks_2Ba* student [maximum_students] ;
```

Here, we define the array called **student** with 10 elements. The array type is **student_marks_2Ba** followed by *. You will recall that when a type is followed by asterisk, this indicates a pointer variable. So, we have an array of 10 pointer variables to the object class **student_marks_2Ba**.

The second data member, `student_index`, is used to store the position in the array of the pointer variable to the last `student_marks_2Ba` object to be added. This will have the value 0 when there is just one object, 1 when there are two objects and so on.

Following the constructor prototype `module_B ()`, we have a similar piece of code.

```
~module_B () ;
```

This is the prototype of a **programmer-defined destructor**. In chapter 10, we briefly mentioned that when the function in which an object is created finishes a default destructor is automatically called to return the memory used by the object. This does not include any additional memory allocated dynamically during the execution of one of the object's member functions. In these cases we must incorporate a programmer-defined destructor. This is declared in the object class definition in the same way as for a constructor except that the identifier is prefixed by the ~ (tilde) character. Also, a destructor does not have arguments.

Figures 14.7 and 14.8 show the constructor and destructor for the `module_B` object class.

```
module_B::module_B ()
   {
   student_index = -1 ;
   for (int counter = 0 ; counter <
      maximum_students ; ++ counter)
      {
      student [counter] = NULL ;
      }
   }
```

Figure 14.7

```
module_B::~module_B ()
   {
   for (int counter = 0 ; counter <=
      student_index ; ++ counter)
      {
      delete student [counter] ;
      }
   }
```

Figure 14.8

In the constructor, we first initialise the member data item `student_index` to -1. We do this because the first index for an array element in C++ is zero, so when we have none we will use -1. Note that we cannot do this as part of the object class definition. The C++ rule is that all initialisation of data members must be done in a constructor. Next, we have a simple **for** loop to initialise the array of pointers so that each element has a value of **NULL**. As with other pointer variables, it is wise to ensure that they contain an initial **NULL** value.

The purpose of the destructor is to ensure that any memory allocated for dynamic objects (this is done in the member function **get_student**) is returned to the memory management system. This is done using the **delete** operator which is executed in a **for** loop.

```
delete student [counter] ;
```

When using pointers to most data types we use the function **free**, as we saw in the previous section, to return memory. For pointers to objects we use the operator **delete** followed by a pointer variable containing the memory address, in this case an element of our pointer array **student**.

The member function **get_student** illustrates the way in which we obtain a dynamic object. It is given in figure 14.9.

```
void module_B::get_student ()
   {
   if (student_index < maximum_students - 1)
      {
      ++ student_index ;
      student [student_index] =
         new student_marks_2Ba ;
      if (student [student_index] == NULL)
         {
         cout << "No memory available" << endl ;
         exit (1) ;
         }
      student [student_index]->display_marks () ;
      }
   else
      cout << "Too many students" << endl ;
   }
```

Figure 14.9

In this function, we first test that we have not already obtained the maximum number of **student_marks_2Ba** objects; we have only allocated sufficient space to store pointers for 10.

Next, after increasing **student_index**, we request memory for and create a dynamic object, then, as in the previous section, check that memory has been allocated.

```
student [student_index] = new student_marks_2Ba ;
if (student [student_index] == NULL)
   {
   cout << "No memory available" << endl ;
   exit (1) ;
   }
```

Here, we use the operator **new** followed by the object class as opposed to the function **malloc** for other data types. This operator causes memory to be allocated to hold an object (of class **student_marks_2Ba**). and store the address in the pointer array element **student [student_index]**. When this is done, the constructor for the object class is called automatically. This invokes the inherited **initialise** function (defined in the base class **student_marks_2B** in **marks2b.h**), the user is prompted for the student and module identity codes and exam and practical marks, that are used to initialise the object.

Once the dynamic object has been created, we use it when calling the member function **display_marks**. We have a new syntax for the function call.

Since **student [student_index]** points to the memory area allocated to the object, we could have called the member function, as in previous examples, by using the dot operator:

```
(*student [student_index]).display_marks () ;
```

For dynamic objects, an easier way to access a particular member is to use the pointer variable followed by the **arrow operator** (->) as in this example:

```
student [student_index]->display_marks () ;
```

The second member function **remove_student** illustrates the way in which we remove a dynamic object. It is given in figure 14.10.

```
void module_B::remove_student ()
   {
   if (student_index >= 0)
      {
      cout << "Student removed" ;
      student [student_index]->
         display_identities () ;
      delete student [student_index] ;
      student [student_index] = NULL ;
      -- student_index ;
      }
   else
      cout << "No students left" << endl ;
   }
```

Figure 14.10

This function is designed to remove the last `student_marks_2Ba` object created. So we must first ensure that there is one by testing `student_index`. Given that there is at least one, we then display the module and student identities of the last object created by using

```
student [student_index]->display_identities () ;
```

We use the current value of `student_index` as an index to the pointer array `student`, then the arrow operator followed by the function call to `display_identities`.

To delete the last object created, we again use the current value of `student_index` as an index to the pointer array `student`. Once we have deleted the object (that is returned its memory to the system), we re-initialise the pointer variable to **NULL** and decrease `student_index`.

When introducing dynamic variables at the start of the previous section, we mentioned that they should be used instead of arrays when, for example, there is a need to store data about an unknown number of students. The use of an array in this example to hold the pointer values for objects is somewhat restrictive and artificial. We need to know the maximum number of objects that are to be used even though we do not have to reserve storage for them at the outset. Ideally we would like to have truly dynamic data storage that does not rely on knowing the maximum number of students. This involves using data structures such as linked lists, stacks or trees that are outside the scope of this book. Happily, most C++ compilers provide container class libraries that provide the necessary facilities.

Finally, consider the program file **array_p.cpp** that makes use of the **module_B** class. This is given in figure 14.11.

The program provides a simple menu system to which the user responds by typing a capital **A** to add a student, **R** to remove a student and **E** to exit from the program. A simplified example of the dialogue produced by the program is shown in figure 14.12.

Note that when **computing.get_student ()** is executed, the data acquisition dialogue between

```
Enter student identity code JK100
```

and

```
Enter next practical mark (or 999) 75
```

is produced by the constructor for `student_marks_2Ba` being called automatically, as explained above, at the statement

```
student [student_index] = new student_marks_2Ba ;
```

The next line in the dialogue: **"Exam mark is 77 Practical mark is 75"**, is produced by

```
student [student_index]->display_marks () ;
```

in the same call to `get_student`.

```
// ARRAY_P.CPP
// Illustrates the use of an array of pointers to
// an object class
#include "module_b.h"
void main ()
   {
   module_B computing ;
   char option,
        terminator ;
   do
      {
      cout << "Enter option: 'A' add a student"
         << endl ;
      cout << "                'R' remove a student"
         << endl ;
      cout << "                'E' end this run"
         << endl ;
      cout << "Enter option: " ;
      cin.get (option) ;
      cin.get (terminator) ;
      if (option == 'A')
         computing.get_student () ;
      else if (option == 'R')
         computing.remove_student () ;
      }
   while (option != 'E') ;
   }
```

Figure 14.11

14.6 Exercises

14.6.1 Please refer to the example in figure 14.1, then answer the following
questions:
(a) Name two local variables. What is the scope of these local
variables?
(b) Name a global constant and a global array. What is their scope?
(c) What is the effect of declaring a variable as **static**?

14.6.2 Please refer to the example in figure 14.2, then answer the following
questions:
(a) Name the object that has global scope. What is its lifetime?

```
Enter option:  'A'  add a student
               'R'  remove a student
               'E'  end this run
Enter option:  R
No students left
Enter option:  'A'  add a student
               'R'  remove a student
               'E'  end this run
Enter option:  A
Enter student identity code JK100
Enter module identity code GEOG
Enter examination mark no. 1 19
Enter examination mark no. 2 15
Enter examination mark no. 3 12
Enter examination mark no. 4 20
Enter examination mark no. 5 11
Enter first practical mark (or 999) 75
Enter next practical mark (or 999) 999
Exam mark is 77 Practical mark is 75
Enter option:  'A'  add a student
               'R'  remove a student
               'E'  end this run
Enter option:  R
Student removed
Student identity:  JK100 for Module:  GEOG
Enter option:  'A'  add a student
               'R'  remove a student
               'E'  end this run
Enter option:  E
```

Figure 14.12

    (b) Name the automatic object that has local scope. What is its lifetime?

    (c) Explain the difference between the declaration of the object **english_JP200** and the object **french_EP100**. What effect does this have on the calls to **display_identities** and **display_marks**?

14.6.3   Please refer to the example in figure 14.4, then answer the following questions:

    (a) How is a pointer variable declared and initialised?

    (b) In general terms, what does the function **malloc** do?

    (c) Why is **int_pointer** tested for a value of **NULL**?

(d) What is the difference between ***int_pointer** and
int_pointer? Use the output of the two **cout** statements to
explain.

14.6.4 Please refer to the examples in figures 14.6 to 14.8, then answer the
following questions:
(a) How do we declare a pointer to an object?
(b) How is a programmer-declared destructor defined?
(c) What is the purpose of the constructor **module_B**?
(d) Why is the destructor **~module_B** necessary?
(e) What does the **delete** operator do?

14.6.5 Please refer to the examples in figures 14.9 and 14.10, then answer the
following questions:
(a) What is the effect of the statement containing the **new** operator?
(b) What is the **->** (arrow) operator used for?
(c) What is the purpose of the five statements associated with the **if**
in the member function **remove_student**?

14.6.6 Make changes as necessary to **module_b.h** in figures 14.6 to 14.10
to achieve the following revised specification.
(a) After a student has been added, the message **"Student added"**
is displayed followed on the next line by the output from the
function **display_identities**.
(b) When **remove_student** is called, the object pointed to in the
first array element is deleted (if there is one). After this, each
pointer should be moved along the array. That is, the one in the
element indexed by 1 should be moved to that indexed by 0, the
one indexed by 2 moved to that indexed by 1 and so on. Finally the
last element is given a null value. Hint: use a **for** loop with a
counter going from 1 to **student_index**.

14.6.7 Produce two header files (**car.h** and **carsales.h**) and a program
file (**assig147.cpp**) to achieve the following specification.

The header file **car.h** has a simple object class definition as
indicated by the model given in figure 14.13 and the pseudo-code in
figure 14.14. The model name is a string with a maximum of 15
characters and the registration mark is a string with a maximum of 7
characters.

A program is required to accept the model name and registration mark
for 10 cars from the keyboard. Then the user is prompted with the
choice of either 'selling' a car or ending the run. If the 'sell' option is
selected, the user is prompted for the registration of the car to be sold.
If the registration is present, the car is deleted and an appropriate
message displayed; otherwise a message indicating that the car could

not be found is displayed. At the end, a list of the cars left in stock is displayed. An abbreviated example dialogue is given in figure 14.15.

The model for the object class **car_sales** is given in figure 14.16, the pseudo-code for **carsales.h** is in figure 14.17 and **assig147.cpp** is in figure 14.18.

In the function **sell_car** you will need to compare strings to determine if the registration mark accepted from the keyboard matches that of the object pointed to in an array element and returned by the member function **return_registration** of the object class **car**. To compare strings in C++, we use the function **strcmp** found in **<string.h>**. This function returns a value of zero if the two strings have the same contents, hence you will need to write a conditional statement such as the following.

```
if (! strcmp (cars_in_stock [car_index]->
    return_registration (), this_registration))
```

Recall that a value of zero may be considered false and a value of non-zero true in a conditional statement. Hence in the above example, if **strcmp** finds the two strings to be the same it returns zero = false.

Class : car
model registration
Get model and registration (constructor) Display model and registration Return registration mark

Figure 14.13

```
car::car
   Declare terminator variable
   Prompt for and accept model name
   Prompt for and accept registration mark

car::display_details
   Display model name and registration mark

char* car::return_registration
   Return registration mark
```

Figure 14.14

```
Enter model name Fiesta 1.3 L
Enter registration P123ABC
 .  .  .
Enter model name Escort 1.5 D
Enter registration R4MO
Enter option: 'S' sell a car
              'E' end this run
Enter option: S
Enter registration of car to be sold A1JAK
Car not found
Enter option: S
Enter registration of car to be sold R4MO
Car sold R4MO
Enter option: 'S' sell a car
              'E' end this run
Enter option: E
Cars left in stock
Model Fiesta 1.3 L Registration P132ABC
 .  .  .
Model Mondeo 1.9 D Registration R999COP
```

Figure 14.15

Class : car_sales
cars_in_stock [10] (of pointers to car)
Get details into array (constructor) Display list from array (destructor) Sell car (remove from array)

Figure 14.16

```
car_sales::car_sales
   FOR counter goes from 0 to 9 in steps of 1
      Create new car object, store pointer in array
         indexed by counter
      IF insufficient memory
         Display message and exit

car_sales::~car_sales
   Display heading "Cars left in stock"
   FOR counter goes from 0 to 9 in steps of 1
      IF array element indexed by counter != NULL
         Call display_details for car object
            pointed to in array indexed by counter
         Delete car object pointed to in array
            element indexed by counter

car_sales::sell_car
   Declare variables
   Prompt for and accept registration mark
   Declare and initialise car index and found (=0)
   WHILE not (found or car index = maximum of 10)
      IF array indexed by car index != NULL
         IF registration mark matches that pointed
            to in array indexed by car index
            Set found = 1
            Display car sold message
            Delete car object pointed to in array
               element indexed by car_index
            Reset array element indexed by
               car index to NULL
      Increase car index by 1
   IF not found
      Display "Car not found"
```

Figure 14.17

```
main
   Declare object ford of type car_sales
   Declare variables
   DO
      Display options and accept user response
      IF response = 'S'
         Call ford.sell_car
   WHILE option != 'E'
```

Figure 14.18

15 Streams and Files

Objectives for this chapter
Familiarity with the C++ programming terms and concepts:
- serial and sequential files
- streams and file streams
- the `ofstream` and `ifstream` classes
- opening and closing files
- the function `eof` (end of file)
- object persistence.

Ability to:
- understand and write simple C++ programs that use file streams.

15.1 Disk files

In all the examples considered so far, input data has been entered at the keyboard and output from the program has been displayed on the monitor screen. However, instead of entering data at the keyboard, we could store the data in a disk file and use this as the input to our program. Also, instead of displaying data on the monitor screen, the program could write the data to a disk file which could be read by the user or processed later by another program.

Computer files on disk can be structured or organised in a variety of ways to facilitate their creation or to enable efficient access to their component parts. As this is rather a large subject we will confine our discussion in this chapter to a description of the most basic and, as it turns out, the most commonly used file structures: serial or sequential files.

Serial or sequential files may consist simply of a number of simple data items, such as integers representing a collection of prices, stored one after the other like music items are stored on an audio cassette.

Alternatively, serial or sequential files may consist of a number of grouped data items called records. For example, a wages file would contain the details of all employees. The details for each employee, such as name, basic wage, hours worked and so on, would be stored together in a record. We refer to these components of a record as fields. When we access this type of file we would normally access a complete record.

When writing to serial or sequential files, it is only possible to write a new data item immediately after the last one already written. Similarly, when reading from serial or sequential files, it is only possible to read the next data item in sequence. Further, once we have read a data item it is impossible to access any of the preceding data items except by closing the file, re-opening it and reading through the file from the beginning.

A serial file is one that has been created with no relationship between its data items or records other than a temporal one; the item written to the file first is placed first, the one written last is placed last. If a serial file contains data items that have been sorted such that there is a relationship between the data items based on the value of one or more key fields, then it becomes a sequential file. For example, if the records in a serial personnel file are sorted into ascending order of employee identification number then it would be known as a sequential file.

15.2 Streams

In C++, input and output to any device whether it be the monitor screen or a disk file are viewed as a stream of characters. Various functions are available in C++ libraries to provide facilities for input and output without the programmer being concerned with the physical aspects of the device. For example, when the user types characters at the keyboard they enter an input stream (an area in memory) waiting for the program to use them. The programmer does not need to know where this stream is held or write special functions to extract the different types of data that might be represented. Data is held in memory in a different form to the way we see it on the monitor screen or in a file. Consequently, for both input and output the data has to be converted from one form to the other, but the programmer does not have to be concerned with this.

In the examples in previous chapters, we have concerned ourselves with input from the keyboard and output to the monitor screen, and have used the two objects `cin` and `cout`. We will now review these and then, in the next section, examine objects for handling disk files.

Consider the following statement.

```
cout << "Enter examination mark no. "
    << question_number << ' ' ;
```

Here, we have a prompt that uses the pre-defined stream object `cout` with its own special operator `<<` (the insertion operator). In fact this operator has multiple uses depending on the operand that follows it. In the above, the first `<<` has a string operand; the specified characters will be displayed on the screen. The second `<<` has an `int` operand; the value of the integer will be converted so that it can be displayed on the screen. The third `<<` has a single character, a space, as its operand; the space will be displayed. Having multiple uses for an operator is called operator overloading; we will discuss this in the next chapter.

Now consider a statement using `cin`.

```
cin >> mark ;
```

Again, `cin` is a pre-defined stream object with its own special operator `>>` (the extraction operator). This operator too has multiple uses depending on the operand that follows it. In the above, if the operand `mark` is of type `int`, then numeric characters will be taken from the input stream and placed in `mark` as an integer value. As well as the obvious conversion that takes place, the process must know how many characters to convert and deal with any white-space characters. (Remember that a white-space character is a blank, a tab, a newline or a carriage return.) It does this by first ignoring any white-space characters then processing the numeric characters up to the next non-numeric character (usually a white-space character). This means that we can process several values in one `cin` statement. For example,

```
cin >> exam_mark >> practical_mark ;
```

If we typed the following characters

		1	3	7	tab		3	5	newline

the first two blanks would be skipped over and the value **137** would be placed in `exam_mark`. Then the tab and the following blank would be ignored and the value **35** placed in `practical_mark`.

If the operand of `>>` is a character or a string of characters, then white-spaces are again ignored. This can be a problem when we wish to read strings with embedded blanks or read a single white-space character. For example, we might type the following as input

	A		b	i	g		h	e	l	l	o	newline

with a program that executes the following statement

```
cin >> character >> message ;
```

where `character` is of type `char` and `message` is a twelve-character string. Now the first blank is skipped, then **A** is placed in `character`. The second blank is skipped and just **big** is placed in `message`. The remaining characters from the third blank onwards would remain in the input stream awaiting further input operations.

To overcome this problem we use the member function `get`:

```
cin.get (character) ;
cin.get (message, 12) ;
```

By using `get`, we obtain the first blank in `character` and the complete string **A big hello** is placed in `message`. As we have previously observed the newline character remains in the input stream.

Notice that `get` has two different forms or signatures; this is an example of an overloaded function. As with overloaded operators, we shall return to this subject in the next chapter.

15.3 File streams

Serial or sequential files are processed as streams in C++, so we use a similar approach to that outlined above when reading from, or writing to, a file. There are some fundamental differences however. First, while there is normally only one keyboard and one monitor screen associated with a program there may be many different files. It is therefore necessary to instantiate stream objects for each file and be able to associate the stream object with the name of the file as known to the computer's operating system. Second, there may be variations in the way in which we use the data in files. For example, we may create a completely new version of an output file, or we may add data to the end of an existing file. Third, when we have finished using a file in a program we should close it to allow other programs or operating system processes to use it.

Let us now look at an example of an object class that has a function that writes data to a file and another function that reads the data from the file. The problem being solved is similar to that used in chapters 11 and 12 on arrays; namely, to display the identity and exam mark of those students whose exam mark is above the average for a particular module. This time we store the data in a file rather than an array. When using an array, the data will be lost once the program finishes. If for any reason, we need to retain certain data values after the program has finished, then obviously we have to write the values to a file as opposed to storing them in an array. The object class is given in diagrammatic form in figure 15.1, the start of the C++ code in **module_c.h** is given in figure 15.2. Note that, as we did in chapter 12 where we used an array of objects, we inherit the object class **student_marks_2Bc** from the header file **marks2bc.h**.

Class : module_C
student (pointer to student_marks_2Bc) average mark

Get student data, write to a file and compute
   the average mark
Read student data from file, display those
   that are above the average
Set average mark to a given number

Figure 15.1

```
// MODULE_C.H
// The object class module_C
#include <fstream.h>
#include <stdlib.h>
#include "marks2bc.h"
class module_C
   {
   public :
      void write_students () ;
      void read_students () ;
      void set_average (int given_average) ;
   protected :
      int average_mark ;
      student_marks_2Bc* student ;
   } ;
```

Figure 15.2

```
module_C::write_students
   Create a new output file stream "student.dat"
   Declare local variables
   Initialise total and count to zero
   DO
      Create new student marks object
      Call initialise for student marks object
      Get exam mark
      Write exam mark student id. to output stream
      Add exam mark to total
      Increase count by 1
      Delete student object
      Prompt for and get repeat request
   WHILE repeat requested
   Compute average mark
   Close output stream
```

Figure 15.3

The function to obtain student data and write it to a file is given as pseudo-code in figure 15.3, the C++ code from **module_c.h** is given in figure 15.4.

The first thing we do in **write_students** is to create a new output file stream for the file to be called **student.dat** by using

```
ofstream output_file ("student.dat") ;
```

```
void module_C::write_students ()
   {
   ofstream output_file ("student.dat") ;
   char repeat_character,
        terminator ;
   int   total = 0 ;
   int   count = 0 ;
   do
      {
      student = new student_marks_2Bc ;
      if (student == NULL)
         {
         cout << "No memory available" << endl ;
         exit (1) ;
         }
      student->initialise () ;
      int exam_mark = student->return_exam_mark () ;
      output_file << exam_mark << ' '
         << student->return_student_identity ()
         << endl ;
      total += exam_mark ;
      ++ count ;
      delete student ;
      cout << "Press A for another, E to end " ;
      cin.get (repeat_character) ;
      cin.get (terminator) ;
      }
   while (repeat_character == 'A') ;
   average_mark = total / count ;
   output_file.close () ;
   }
```

Figure 15.4

Here we instantiate an object of the **ofstream** class found in the header file **fstream.h** and open a new output file of the specified name. Alternatively, we could have instantiated the object and used the **open** function to open the file:

```
ofstream output_file ;
output_file.open ("student.dat") ;
```

Either way, we need to specify a parameter containing the file name; this associates the programmer-chosen name for the object, **output_file**, with the name of the file as known to the operating system, **student.dat**.

Also, because there are a number of different modes of opening a file, there is a second parameter, the opening mode, which may be specified as an integer value or by system specified constant values. We have not used it here as the default value is to open a new file for output, that is for writing to.

The different opening modes are given in figure 15.5 together with the integer values that would be used as the second parameter.

Opening Mode	Integer Parameter Value
open for reading	1
open for writing	2
open and move to end of file	4
append additions at end of file	8
if file already exists delete contents	16
if file does not exist, fail on open	32
if file already exists, fail on open	64

Figure 15.5

After creating a new object in memory and calling the initialise function for it, the exam mark is obtained by using the **return_exam_mark** function. The next statement puts the exam mark and the student identity into the output file stream.

```
output_file << exam_mark << ' '
    << student->return_student_identity ()
    << endl ;
```

Notice that the format is the same as when using **cout**, we use the << operator for each item to be placed in the stream: an integer value from **exam_mark**, followed by a single space character (to act as a separator), followed by the string that represents the student identity returned from the **return_student_identity** function, followed by an end of line (newline) symbol.

If two student objects were created in the **do-while** loop, the output stream would contain the following with a stream pointer positioned after the second newline ready for subsequent items.

3	5		M	K	1	0	0	newline	7	1		J	P	2	1	5	newline

When the user chooses to type any character other than the letter A at the repeat request prompt, the loop is terminated and the average mark is computed. Then the file stream is closed by

```
output_file.close () ;
```

This has been included to demonstrate the function even though in this particular case it is not necessary to close the output file stream. This is because at this point the **write_students** function would be terminated and the object **output_file** would fall out of scope. Hence the destructor for `output_file` would be called automatically and this in turn would call the `close` function as required. The effect of `close` for an output file is to ensure that all of the stream data has been written to the output file and that the file is returned to the control of the operating system so that it can be used by other processes. The file `student.dat` would then contain

```
35 MK100
71 JP215
```

The function to read this file and display those students with an exam mark above the average is given as pseudo-code in figure 15.6. This illustrates the 'read-ahead' technique, first introduced in chapter 8 (see figure 8.9), that proves very useful when processing data from an input file.

```
module_C::read_students
    Declare local variables
    Create an input file stream for "student.dat"
    Read first exam mark
    Display heading
    WHILE not at the end of the input stream
        Skip over separator
        Read student identity
        IF exam mark > average mark
            Display student identity and exam mark
        Read next exam mark
    Close input stream
```

Figure 15.6

Notice in particular the position of the read statements. We attempt to read an exam mark before we enter the **WHILE** loop and as the last statement within the loop. If either read is unsuccessful because we are already at the end of the file stream then the end of file stream state is set accordingly and we are able to test that state in the condition that controls the loop. This technique is necessary because the end of input file stream state is only set when we have already read the last item in the file and another attempt to read from it is made, so we must attempt to read before we can test for end of input. It is also convenient, because it allows for the situation when we have an empty file.

The other two read statements are used once only within the loop and follow logically after a successful read of an exam mark; a space as a separator and a student identity string must follow an exam mark.

The C++ code for the function `read_students` from `module_c.h` is given in figure 15.7.

First, we note the creation of the input file stream object by

```
ifstream input_file ("student.dat") ;
```

Here we instantiate an object of the **ifstream** class as opposed to the

```
void module_C::read_students ()
   {
   char identity [9] ;
   int  exam_mark ;
   char separator ;
   ifstream input_file ("student.dat") ;
   if (! input_file)
      {
      cout << "Student file not available" << endl ;
      exit (1) ;
      }
   input_file >> exam_mark ;
   cout << endl << "Students with merits" << endl ;
   while (! input_file.eof())
      {
      input_file.get (separator) ;
      input_file.get (identity, 9) ;
      if (exam_mark > average_mark)
         cout << "Student " << identity << "\t"
            << setw (3) << exam_mark << endl ;
      input_file >> exam_mark ;
      }
   input_file.close () ;
   }
```

Figure 15.7

ofstream class that we used for an output file. This creates the object and opens an input file of the specified name. Again, we could have instantiated the object and used the **open** function to open the file:

```
ifstream input_file ;
input_file.open ("student.dat") ;
```

As with the output file, we specify the file name as the first parameter and may use an integer value to specify an opening mode as an optional second parameter. There is no need for the integer parameter in this case because the default is to open a file that already exists for reading.

In this example, we are quite sure that we will always have **student.dat** available because we will always use the function **write_students** before using **read_students**. However, it is good practice to guard against the possible error situation where the input file may not be available to the program. We do so by implementing code such as below.

```
if (! input_file)
   {
```

```
cout << "Student file not available" << endl ;
exit (1) ;
}
```

We may test the state of the object as above. If it is true, the file has been opened correctly, if false, it has not. Here, if false, we simply display an error message then issue an **exit** statement to exit from the program.

The syntax for reading items from the file stream is exactly as for **cin**. We may use the operator >> as well as the **ifstream** member function **get**. We use the former to obtain an exam mark by

```
input_file >> exam_mark ;
```

and the latter to skip over the separator and obtain the student identity string by

```
input_file.get (separator) ;
input_file.get (identity, 9) ;
```

Since objects of the **ifstream** class interpret input exactly the same way as **cin**, the two statements above could be replaced by

```
input_file >> identity ;
```

provided there are no spaces in the identity.

To detect the end of the input stream, we use the member function **eof** (end of file) as follows

```
while (! input_file.eof())
```

If the stream pointer has reached the end of the input stream and an attempt is made to read another value, true is returned otherwise false.

One further point from the example is demonstrated in the code that displays the student identity and exam mark:

```
cout << "Student " << identity << "\t"
     << setw (3) << exam_mark << endl ;
```

The output produced here will be tabulated such that the exam marks will always be vertically aligned, even though the string **identity** may vary in length for different students. The control character "**\t**" (tab) causes the screen cursor to be moved to the next horizontal tabulation position.

A simple program **merits2.cpp** is given in figure 15.8 to illustrate how the object class **module_C** may be used.

Figure 15.9 is an example of the dialogue produced on the monitor screen when the program is executed. The interactive acquisition of the student and module identities and the exam and practical marks is produced by repeatedly calling the function **initialise** within the **do-while** loop of **write_students**. The list at the end is produced by the call to **read_students**.

After **merits2.cpp** has executed there will remain a file called **student.dat** containing some of the member data, **exam_mark** and **student_identity**, of the **student_marks_2Bc** objects created in

```
// MERITS2.CPP
// A program to get exam marks for a number of
// students and display those that are above the
// average
#include "module_c.h"
void main ()
    {
    module_C computing ;
    computing.write_students () ;
    computing.read_students () ;
    }
```

Figure 15.8

```
Enter student identity code MK321
Enter module identity code COMP
Enter examination mark no. 1 17
. . .
Enter examination mark no. 5 18
Enter first practical mark (or 999) 999
Press A for another, E to end A
. . .
. . .
Enter student identity code JK456
Enter module identity code COMP
Enter examination mark no. 1 12
. . .
Enter examination mark no. 5 7
Enter first practical mark (or 999) 999
Press A for another, E to end E

Students with merits
Student MK321      80
Student EP582      92
```

Figure 15.9

write_students. We can illustrate this by executing another program,
merits3.cpp, given in figure 15.10.

Here we create a module_C object then use the function set_average
to give the data member average_mark a value of 20. The member function
set_average, from module_c.h, is given in figure 15.11.

Having already stored the exam_mark and student_identity for a
number of students in student.dat, we can then call the read_students

```
// MERITS3.CPP
// A program to display marks above 20% from the
// file student.dat
#include "module_c.h"
void main ()
    {
    module_C computing ;
    computing.set_average (20) ;
    computing.read_students () ;
    }
```

Figure 15.10

```
void module_C::set_average (int given_average)
    {
    average_mark = given_average ;
    }
```

Figure 15.11

member function to read the file and hence display the identity and exam mark
of those that have got more than 20%.

Note that we cannot directly access **average_mark** here because it is a
protected data member of **module_C**. We could have made it a **public**
member to facilitate this, but normally it is not considered good practice to
allow public access to data members; rather we should always use functions to
set the values of data members or, as we have already seen, to return the values
of data members (for example, **return_student_identity**).

15.4 Object persistence

In previous chapters, we have considered objects that exist only during the
execution of the program in which they are defined. Such objects are known as
transient objects. The lifetime of transient objects ends when a program
completes and is unloaded from computer memory.

Persistent objects exist between program runs; their lifetime extends
beyond the end of a single program execution. For an object to be persistent, it
must be stored in a disk file. Strictly, it is not possible to store everything about
an object using a disk file that is organised in a standard way. However, it is
possible to store the state of an object as represented by the current values of an
object's member data. From the stored data it is possible to recreate the state of
such an object although strictly this would mean creating a new one and using a
mechanism to reinitialise the member data values to those stored in the disk
file.

In the previous section we have demonstrated in a simplified way how the values held in the member data of objects may be stored in a disk file, then how that data may be retrieved and used. Some of the member data of the **student_marks_2Bc** objects, created when **merits2.cpp** was run, persisted beyond the execution of that program and were then used in **merits3.cpp**.

15.5 Exercises

15.5.1   Please refer to sections 15.1 and 15.2, then answer the following questions:

(a) What is the difference between a serial disk file and a sequential disk file?

(b) Why is **cin.get (character)** sometimes used in preference to **cin >> character**?

(c) Why is **cin.get (message, 12)** sometimes used in preference to **cin >> message**?

15.5.2   Please refer to the example in figure 15.4, then answer the following questions:

(a) Give two ways of creating and opening a file stream for output.

(b) What is an opening mode?

(c) Why is **output_file.close ()** not necessary in the **write_students** function?

(d) What is the difference in the way in which we actually write output to a a disk file as opposed to the monitor screen?

(e) Can you suggest a reason for writing the blank character between the exam mark and the student identity? Is it necessary?

15.5.3   Please refer to the example in figures 15.6 and 15.7, then answer the following questions:

(a) Why is the technique of reading the exam mark before entering the loop and as the last statement within the body of the loop necessary?

(b) What beneficial effect does the above technique also provide?

(c) Give two ways of creating and opening a file stream for input.

(d) Why is it usually necessary to use the statement
if (! input_file)?

(e) How do we detect the end of the input file stream?

15.5.4   Please refer to the start of section 15.3 and section 15.4, then answer the following questions.

(a) What are three fundamental differences that should be noted when using disk files for input and output as opposed to the keyboard and monitor screen?

(b) What is a persistent object and how is object persistence normally implemented?

(c) Explain why an array cannot be used to implement object persistence.

15.5.5   Make changes as necessary to **module_c.h** in figures 15.2, 15.4 and 15.7 to achieve the following revised specification.

(a) Remove all references to the average mark and its evaluation.

(b) Write the practical mark to **student.dat** between the exam mark and the student identity. You may assume the function **return_practical_mark** of the object class **student_marks_2Bc**.

(c) Change the **read_students** function so that it displays the student identity, exam mark and practical mark of those students that have achieved over 50% in both the exam mark and the practical mark.

15.5.6   Produce a header file (**ages.h**) and a program file (**assig156.cpp**) to achieve the specification described by the model in figure 15.12, the pseudo-code in figures 15.13 and 15.14 and the sample dialogue in figure 15.15.

Write another program file (**assig157.cpp**) that will now use the data in the file **ages.dat** to display the table up to a maximum age of 15 as opposed to 21 in the first program.

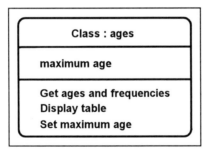

Figure 15.12

```
ages::get_ages_and_frequencies
   Create a new output file stream "ages.dat"
   Declare local variables
   FOR age from 1 to 25 in steps of 1
      Prompt for and accept frequency
      IF frequency not zero
         Write age and frequency to output stream
   Close output stream

ages::display_table
   Declare local variables
   Display headings
   Create an input file stream for "ages.dat"
   Read first age from input stream
   WHILE not end of stream and age <= maximum age
      Read frequency from input stream
      Display age and frequency
      Read next age from input stream
   Close input stream

ages::set_maximum_age (given age)
   Assign given age to maximum age
```

Figure 15.13

```
main
   Create object horses of type ages
   Call horses.get_ages_and_frequencies
   Call horses.set_maximum_age (21)
   Call horses.display_table
```

Figure 15.14

```
Enter frequency for age 1 0
Enter frequency for age 2 0
Enter frequency for age 3 20
Enter frequency for age 4 0
Enter frequency for age 5 23
.  .  .
Enter frequency for age 25 0

TABLE OF ACCIDENT FREQUENCIES BY AGE UP TO AGE 21

    3 years            20
    5 years            23
   12 years            24
   ...
   21 years            36
```

Figure 15.15

16 Introduction to Polymorphism

Objectives for this chapter
Familiarity with the C++ programming terms and concepts:
- operator overloading
- operator functions
- function overloading
- a signature
- **friend** functions
- using more than one constructor in a single object class
- parametric polymorphism and templates
- generic functions.

Ability to:
- understand the fundamentals of polymorphism and use some of the C++ language constructs that support them.

16.1 What is polymorphism?

Polymorphism literally means "having many forms". In C++, both operators and functions can have many forms in that they can be adapted so that while the meaning of their operation is the same their implementation will allow for their use with different types of data. In practice, this means that we can use both operators and function names to achieve different things depending on the context in which they are used.

It is not possible, nor even desirable, to discuss all of the different types of polymorphism in an introductory book. For this reason, we will just introduce some of the fundamental concepts using simple illustrative examples.

16.2 Operator overloading

We have seen that the arithmetic operators work with both `int` and `float` values. For example,

```
int    integer_number = 23 + 51 ;
float real_number = 5.7 + 7.2 ;
```

are both normal expressions using the + operator. However, it is apparent that the + operator is doing two different jobs depending on its context. If its operands are of type **int** it performs integer arithmetic, if its operands are of type **float** it does real arithmetic. Similarly, the insertion operator, <<, used with **cout** performs different output conversions depending on the type of its operand. For example,

```
cout << integer_number << " - " << real_number ;
```

would output the first value according to the rules for the output of values of type **int**, then a string of 3 characters, then the real number according to the rules for the output of values of type **float**.

These examples illustrate that operators must, in many situations, be capable of a form of polymorphism; in the above cases, the ability to perform the same operation, addition and output, on different types of data.

Further, in C++, there are a number of operators that combine two operands and allow each operand to be of a different data type. For example,

```
real_number = integer_number + 5.75 ;
```

is evaluated by first converting the value in **integer_number** to a **float** value then using real arithmetic to produce the required **float** result. This process is called **coercion** and will occur according to rules built into the C++ language for operations with operands of different types.

Sometimes, we need to change the rules by imposing a conversion on an expression or a single variable. We do this by using a **type cast**. For example,

```
float real_number = 3.5 ;
cout << real_number << ' ' << int (real_number) <<
     ' ' << int (real_number + 0.5) << endl ;
```

will output

```
3.5 3 4
```

that is, the original real value, the truncated integer value and the rounded value. The integer values are produced by imposing a type cast on the expression, achieved by preceding the expression by the type **int**.

The assignment operator is overloaded to allow the assignment of many different data types. This also includes the assignment of objects. For example, we can make a copy of all of the attributes of an object by:

```
student_marks_2B first_student,
                 second_student ;
first_student.initialise () ;
second_student =  first_student ;
```

All corresponding data members in **second_student** will now contain the same values that were given to **first_student** when **initialise** was called.

This facility to overload the assignment operator is provided by the C++

compiler. However, it is possible for a programmer to produce an operator function that defines another way of assigning one object to another. Also, we may wish to use other operators whose operands are objects. To do this we must define our own overloaded version(s) of such operators using the **operator function** facility.

16.3 Operator functions

Let us suppose that we wanted to compare objects. Continuing our student marks theme, we may wish to establish which student is 'best'. It would be convenient to be able to use the relational operator > to compare two objects. Of course, we would need to define what we mean by greater than in terms of the attributes of the object class.

Let us consider another derived class of **student_marks_2B**, shown in figure 16.1, that illustrates one way in which we may implement an overloaded relational operator for objects.

```
// MARKS2BD.H
// The object class student_marks_2Bd
#include "marks2b.h"
class student_marks_2Bd : public student_marks_2B
   {
   public :
      friend int operator > (student_marks_2Bd
         student_1, student_marks_2Bd student_2) ;
   } ;

int operator > (student_marks_2Bd student_1,
   student_marks_2Bd student_2)
   {
   if (student_1.exam_mark > student_2.exam_mark)
      return 1 ;
   else
      return 0 ;
   }
```

Figure 16.1

We inherit all of **student_marks_2B** and add just one new function known as a **friend** function. Note the rather different prototype.

```
friend int operator > (student_marks_2Bd student_1,
   student_marks_2Bd student_2) ;
```

First, we have the keyword **friend** before the result type **int**. Then we have the keyword **operator** followed by the operator designation >. Two parameters are specified, both of the object class **student_marks_2Bd**.

A friend function does not belong to an object class so it does not have a scope resolution operator in its definition. However, it does have access to the data members of the class in which it is declared as friend.

The function definition for **operator** > simply compares the exam mark of the object that is its first parameter with the exam mark of the object that is its second parameter:

```
if (student_1.exam_mark > student_2.exam_mark)
    return 1 ;
else
    return 0 ;
```

So, we have defined what we mean by an object of type **student_marks_2Bd** being greater than another object of that type. We return 1 (true) or 0 (false).

We use instances of **student_marks_2Bd** and **operator** > in a program to determine which of a number of student marks is best (assuming there is only one). The pseudo-code for the program is given in figure 16.2 and the program file **top_stud.cpp** is given in figure 16.3.

```
main
    Declare variables including best student object
    Call initialise for best student
    DO
        Declare current student object
        Call initialise for current student
        IF current student > best student
            Copy current student into best student
        Prompt for and accept repeat request
    WHILE repeat request = A
    Display "The best student is:"
    Call display_identities for best student
```

Figure 16.2

Here we first create an instance of **student_marks_2Bd** called **best_student** which is initialised using the inherited function **initialise**. Then, in a loop, we create and initialise further instances of **student_marks_2Bd** (called **student**) that are then compared in turn with **best_student**. If **student** is better (greater), then it is copied into **best_student**. When the loop terminates (the user types any other character than A), The identities of the **best_student** are displayed.

In this simple example the condition could just as easily be expressed as:

```
if (student.return_exam_mark () >
    best_student.return_exam_mark ())
```

```
// TOP_STUD.CPP
// A program to get a number of marks and display
// the best student
#include "marks2Bd.h"
void main ()
    {
    char repeat_character,
         terminator ;
    student_marks_2Bd best_student ;
    best_student.initialise () ;
    do
        {
        student_marks_2Bd student ;
        student.initialise () ;
        if (student > best_student)
           best_student = student ;
        cout << "Press A for another, E to end " ;
        cin.get (repeat_character) ;
        cin.get (terminator) ;
        }
    while (repeat_character == 'A') ;
    cout << "The best student is:" ;
    best_student.display_identities () ;
    }
```

Figure 16.3

assuming that we have the required function described in previous examples. But the definition of what constitutes a better **student_marks** object could well be much more complicated and in such cases it would be better if the complexity was 'hidden' in the operator function allowing the simplicity of coding demonstrated in our example to be used elsewhere in the program file.

16.4 Function overloading

A number of library functions exhibit the characteristics of polymorphism in that they are able to operate on different types of data. For example the maths functions **pow** and **sqrt** will work with both **int** and **float** parameters.

We can construct our own overloaded functions. Consider the example given in figure 16.4 (**examp16a.h**) and figure 16.5 (**overload.cpp**).

In this example, we have three different implementations of the member function **display**, designed to handle three different data types in an appropriate way. When the program is run we would get the following output on the monitor screen:

```
// EXAMP16A.H
// The object class examp16a
#include <iostream.h>
#include <iomanip.h>
class examp16a
    {
    public :
       void display (int integer) ;
       void display (float real) ;
       void display (char character) ;
    } ;

void examp16a::display (int integer)
    {
    cout << "Integer output: " << integer << endl ;
    }

void examp16a::display (float real)
    {
    cout << "Real output: " << setprecision (3)
       << real << endl ;
    }

void examp16a::display (char character)
    {
    cout << "Character output: " << character
       << endl ;
    }
```

Figure 16.4

```
// OVERLOAD.CPP
// A sample program to demonstrate an overloaded
// function with three implementations
#include "examp16a.h"
void main ()
    {
    examp16a example ;
    char letter = 'A' ;
    int integer_number = 23 ;
    float real_number = 56.825 ;
    example.display (letter) ;
    example.display (integer_number) ;
    example.display (real_number) ;
    }
```

Figure 16.5

```
Character output: A
Integer output: 23
Real output: 56.825
```

The correct output is produced because of the compiler's ability to distinguish between the three different versions of **display**. It does this by recognising that each implementation has a different **signature** in this case characterised by the type of the parameter.

In chapter 10 it was mentioned that a programmer may write one or more constructors for an object class. Since each constructor must have the identifier of the class to which it belongs, the facility for overloading functions is clearly needed to accomplish this.

We can demonstrate the use of two constructors in a single object class by making minor changes to the example in the previous section, that of determining the 'best' student. Consider the revised header file (**marks2be.h**), given in figure 16.6 and the revised program file (**top_stu2.cpp**), given in figure 16.7.

In the program file in figure 16.7, we notice two declarations of the object class **student_marks_2Be**:

```
student_marks_2Be best_student (0) ;
```
and
```
student_marks_2Be student ;
```

The difference in signature is obvious, the first has a parameter, the second does not. The compiler would have no difficulty when creating the objects in applying the correct constructor. The first declaration would cause the invocation of the constructor that is defined second in the header file:

```
student_marks_2Be::student_marks_2Be
   (int initial_mark)
   {
   exam_mark = initial_mark ;
   }
```

So the data member **exam_mark** would be given a value of 0. The second declaration would cause the first constructor to be used and the function initialise to be called:

```
student_marks_2Be::student_marks_2Be ()
   {
   initialise () ;
   }
```

The net result of these changes is that the object **best_student** is first given a default value of zero for the exam mark rather than being initialised in full as in the original example. Within the loop an object **student** is then initialised in the more usual way upon creation using a constructor calling **initialise**. When the two objects are first compared, since the exam mark in **best_student** is zero, **student** will be assigned to **best_student**.

```
// MARKS2BE.H
// The object class student_marks_2Be
#include "marks2b.h"
class student_marks_2Be : public student_marks_2B
   {
   public :
      friend int operator > (student_marks_2Be
         student_1, student_marks_2Be student_2) ;
      student_marks_2Be () ;
      student_marks_2Be (int initial_mark) ;
   } ;

student_marks_2Be::student_marks_2Be ()
   {
   initialise () ;
   }

student_marks_2Be::student_marks_2Be
   (int initial_mark)
   {
   exam_mark = initial_mark ;
   }

int operator > (student_marks_2Be student_1,
   student_marks_2Be student_2)
   {
   if (student_1.exam_mark > student_2.exam_mark)
      return 1 ;
   else
      return 0 ;
   }
```

Figure 16.6

16.5 Generic functions

Generic functions facilitate polymorphism by providing a single implementation for all data types. This is achieved by building **templates**. For example,
we could write a simple generic function to return the greater of two items. The
items could be any data type including objects for which the operator > is
defined.

Consider the template, defined in its own header file **examp16b.h**, given
in figure 16.8.

```
// TOP_STU2.CPP
// A program to get a number of marks and display
// the best student
#include "marks2be.h"
void main ()
    {
    char repeat_character,
        terminator ;
    student_marks_2Be best_student (0) ;
    do
        {
        student_marks_2Be student ;
        if (student > best_student)
            best_student = student ;
        cout << "Press A for another, E to end " ;
        cin.get (repeat_character) ;
        cin.get (terminator) ;
        }
    while (repeat_character == 'A') ;
    cout << "The best student is:" ;
    best_student.display_identities () ;
    }
```

Figure 16.7

```
// EXAMP16B.H
// A template for functions to return the greater
// of two items
template <class T> T greater (T first, T second)
    {
    if (first > second)
        return first ;
    else
        return second ;
    }
```

Figure 16.8

The template definition must begin with the keyword **template** followed by the template parameter in angular brackets, **<>**. In this case, there is only one argument a type name **T** identified by the keyword **class**. We use **T** by convention (it could be any name); it is an alias for any data type. There follows the function result type, the generic data type **T**, followed by the template function identifier, **greater**, followed by the function parameters:

first and **second** of the generic data type T.

The body of the template function is much the same as any simple function. In this case the two function parameters are compared and the one that is greater is returned as the function result.

Now let us see how we can use this template function in a simple program that processes two integers. The program is in the file **generic.cpp**, given in figure 16.9.

```
// GENERIC.CPP
// Uses template to demonstrate comparison of
// two integers
#include <iostream.h>
#include "examp16b.h"
void main ()
    {
    int first_integer,
        second_integer ;
    cout << "Please enter two integer values: " ;
    cin >> first_integer >> second_integer ;
    cout << "Greater of the two integers is " <<
        greater (first_integer, second_integer)
        << endl ;
    }
```

Figure 16.9

When the program is compiled, a version of **greater** is generated that uses the template and an understanding of the way in which two integers may be compared using the operator > (that is the standard way built into the compiler). The output when the program is executed is:

```
Please enter two integer values: 65 43
Greater of the two integers is 65
```

To demonstrate the genericity of the template function, we can also use it in another simple program that now processes two objects of type **student_marks_2Be**, which you will recall has the operator > defined for it. This program is in the file **generic2.cpp** and is given in figure 16.10.

This time a different version of **greater** is generated by the compiler using the template and a different understanding of the > operator as defined in the object class **student_marks_2Be**. The output (abbreviated) from this program is given in figure 16.11.

When the objects are created, the constructor without a parameter is called and the dialogue to initialise their data members occurs. When **greater** is called, the operator function **operator >**, defined in the class definition, is used to return the 'greater' of the two objects.

```
// GENERIC2.CPP
// Uses template to demonstrate comparison of
// two objects
#include "examp16b.h"
#include "marks2be.h"
void main ()
    {
    student_marks_2Be first_student,
                      second_student ;
    cout << endl << "The better student is:" ;
    greater (first_student,
        second_student).display_identities () ;
    }
```

Figure 16.10

```
Enter student identity code MK234
Enter module identity code BIOL
Enter examination mark no. 1 18
. . .
Enter examination mark no. 5 12
Enter first practical mark (or 999) 999
Enter student identity code JP600
Enter module identity code BIOL
Enter examination mark no. 1 13
. . .
Enter examination mark no. 5 10
Enter first practical mark (or 999) 999

The better student is:
Student identity: MK234 for Module: BIOL
```

Figure 16.11

16.6 Exercises

16.6.1 Please refer to section 16.2, then answer the following questions.
(a) In what way is the + operator overloaded?
(b) What is coercion?
(c) What is a type cast? Under what circumstances do you think we might need to use a type cast?
(d) Describe the way in which the overloading of the assignment operator can be useful in object oriented programming.

16.6.2   Please refer to the example in figures 16.1 to 16.3, then answer the
following questions.
(a) Describe the components of the prototype for the operator function >.
(b) Where is a friend function declared as `friend`? Does it belong to
an object class?
(c) Give the C++ code for a new version of the function `operator >`
that satisfies the specification: an object of class
`student_marks_2Bd` is greater than another if the practical
mark is higher and the examination mark is not zero.

16.6.3   Please refer to the example in figures 16.4 and 16.5, then answer the
following questions.
(a) What output would be displayed for:
```
example.display ('B') ;
```
(b) How does the compiler distinguish between the three versions of
the function `display`?

16.6.4   Please refer to the example in figures 16.6 and 16.7, then answer the
following questions.
(a) How does the compiler distinguish between the two constructors?
(b) What would be the effect of the following in `top_stu2.cpp`?
```
student_marks_2Be excellent_student (100) ;
```

16.6.5   Please refer to the examples in figures 16.8 to 16.10, then answer the
following questions.
(a) Describe the five components of the template definition header?
(b) What must be defined for a data type or object so that it can be
used with the template `greater`?

16.6.6   Make changes as necessary to the example in figures 16.1 and 16.3 so
that the worst student's identities are displayed. The worst student is
the one with the lowest practical mark and you may assume that there
is only one.

16.6.7   Make changes as necessary to the example in figures 16.4 and 16.5 to
include a further version of `display` that will output a character then
an integer then a real number on three lines in the same format as for
the existing versions. Hint: call the existing versions of `display`.

16.6.8   Produce a header file (`temp168.h`) containing a template for
functions that will return the highest value of three items (you may
assume that all three values are different). Demonstrate the use of this
template by producing a program file (`assig168.cpp`) that prompts
for and accepts three integers and displays the one with the highest
value, then creates three `student_marks_2Be` objects and displays
the identities for the 'best' student.

Appendix A : Object Classes Used in Examples

A model and corresponding object class for a student's performance (examination and practical mark) in a subject (module) is introduced in chapter 5. This model is developed and refined in subsequent chapters.

This appendix contains a diagram showing all the object classes that are eventually used and the relationship between them. The diagram also indicates where each class is first introduced in the text enabling the reader to refer back, if necessary, for the full specification.

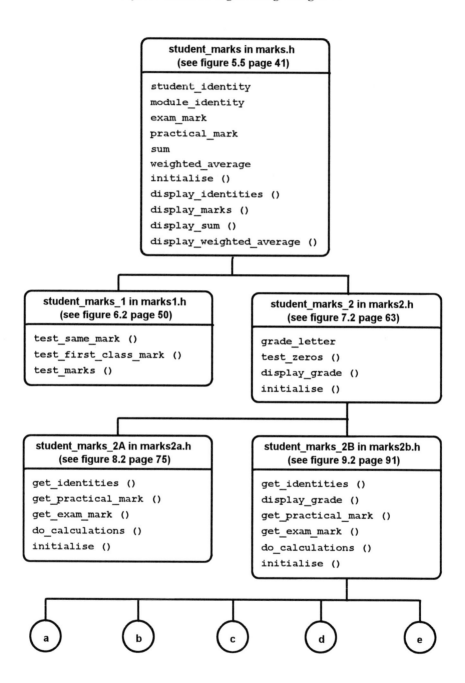

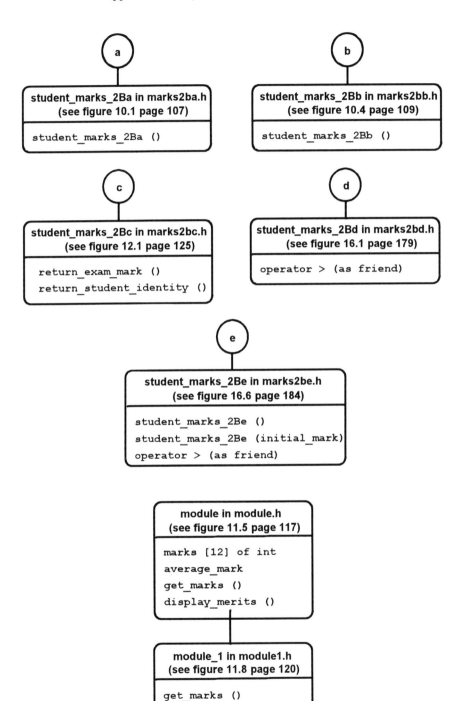

```
+---------------------------------------------------+
|            module_A in module_a.h                 |
|            (see figure 12.3 page 126)             |
+---------------------------------------------------+
| mark_table [12] of student_marks_2Bc              |
| average_mark                                      |
| get_marks ()                                      |
| display_merits ()                                 |
+---------------------------------------------------+
```

```
        +-------------------------------------+
        |          course in course.h         |
        |       (see figure 13.6 page 135)    |
        +-------------------------------------+
        |  marks [4][6] of int                |
        |  get_marks ()                       |
        |  display_marks ()                   |
        +-------------------------------------+
```

```
+-----------------------------------------------------------+
|                 module_B in module_b.h                    |
|                 (see figure 14.6 page 150)                |
+-----------------------------------------------------------+
| student [10] of pointer to student_marks_2Ba              |
| student_index                                             |
| module_B ()                                               |
| ~module_B ()                                              |
| get_student ()                                            |
| remove_student ()                                         |
+-----------------------------------------------------------+
```

```
+-----------------------------------------------------+
|              module_C in module_c.h                 |
|              (see figure 15.2 page 165)             |
+-----------------------------------------------------+
| student (pointer to student_marks_2Bc)              |
| average_mark                                        |
| write_students ()                                   |
| read_students ()                                    |
| set_average (given_average)                         |
+-----------------------------------------------------+
```

Appendix B : Solutions to Exercises

Chapter 1

1.12.1

(a) Compilation of a computer program is the computer process of translating the source code produced by the programmer into the machine code as understood by the electronics of the computer.

(b) An identifier is the name given by a programmer to an item of data in a computer program.

(c) A data type is the specification of a kind of data, such as character or whole number, and its range of acceptable values.

(d) A variable is a named storage area of a particular data type whose value may be changed a number of times during the execution of a program.

(e) The keyboard buffer is a small piece of computer memory into which the values of the keys that are pressed are placed pending their transfer to a computer program's memory.

1.12.2

(a) By a programmer-chosen identifier.

(b) The usual pre-defined data types are: integer, real (or float), character and string.

(c) An assignment statement is a program instruction that changes the value of a variable.

1.12.3

(a) The user requirements specification is a document which describes in precise terms what is required of a computer system. It is produced after consultation with the probable eventual users of the system to explore the current and future requirements in a specific business or technical area.

(b) Pseudo-code is a notation used to describe programs or functions. It contains normal language statements to describe the actions required, and also control statements to indicate the logic.

(c) Testing is the activity of trying to discover errors that may exist in a computer program.

(d) A computer program is reliable if it always produces predictable results on different sets of data.

1.12.4

(a) Problems at one stage might lead back to a previous stage or stages. For example, the testing stage if not completed to the developer's satisfaction could require adjustments at the programming stage.

(b) Syntax errors may occur when a program is compiled. Run-time and logical errors may occur when testing a program.

(c) Debugging.

(d) User documentation is information that explains how to use the program. Technical documentation should contain sufficient datail to enable those responsible for maintaining the software to make changes when necessary.

(e) Corrective, adaptive, perfective and preventive maintenance.

(f) Nearly all computer programs will require some modification, or maintenance, during their lifetime. To be modifiable the end product must be easy to understand.

Chapter 2

2.7.1

(a) A group of objects having the same characteristics (data and behaviour).

(b) Functions define the behaviour of an object class. Each function includes the actions required to achieve a specific task.

(c) An item of data that is part of an object class and describes something about it.

(d) Using the data and behaviour of one object class in the production of a derived class.

(e) Defining the data and behaviour of an object class at one time in a single definition.

2.7.2

(a) A variable has a type that describes its characteristics. An object has an object class that describes its characteristics.

(b) Descendant or child classes.

(c) A piece of software whose users know what it does but not necessarily how it does it.

2.7.3

(a) name, date of birth, qualifications, telephone number (and others not named).

(b) name of secretary, number of staff and others, such as incentive bonus, company car details etc.

(c) office worker, technician, clerk, and many others.

2.7.4

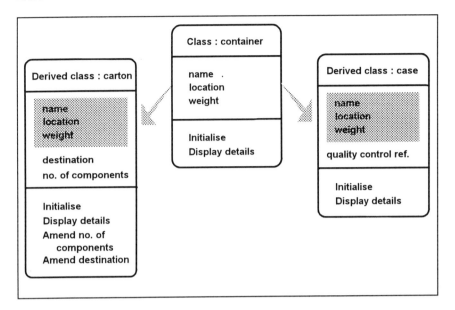

Chapter 3

3.5.1

    (a) Lines 1 and 2 are C++ comments. Their purpose is to describe the program to the human reader. If they were removed, it would have no effect on the running of the program.

    (b) Lines 3 and 4 permit the use of screen output, keyboard input and strings.

    (c) Lines 8 and 9 are member function prototypes. The first part identifies the result type, the second part is the function identifier (name) and the third part is called the function arguments.

    (d) The identifying name is **contents**, it will be used to store characters, to a maximum length of 12 including the end of string character.

    (e) In the function heading, the identifier is preceded by the object class identifier and the resolution operator. Also, there is no semicolon at the end of the function heading.

    (f) The characters **Hello World** are stored in **contents**.

    (g) The string stored in **contents** will be displayed on the monitor screen and then the cursor will be placed at the start of the next line.

    (h) It indicates the point in the file at which program execution begins.

    (i) Line 26 declares an object as an instance of the class **message** giving it the identifier **hello**.

(j) The first component is **hello** which identifies the object of the class **message**. The second is the dot operator (**.**). The third is the member function identifier (**initialise** or **display**). The fourth is the empty argument list (the open and close parentheses).

(k) The statement(s) within the function definition are executed.

(l) **message, initialise, display, contents** and **hello**. Normally an identifier will not exceed 30 characters. It must start with either a letter of the alphabet or the underscore character, with its remaining characters being letters, digits or underscore characters. Keywords must not be used as identifiers.

(m) To allow their use in a function that does not belong to the object class message.

3.5.2

```
// MESSAGES.CPP
// A program to display two messages
#include <iostream.h>
#include <string.h>
class message
    {
    public :
        void initialise () ;
        void display () ;
    protected :
        char contents_1 [25] ;
        char contents_2 [17] ;
    } ;

void message::initialise () ;
    {
    strcpy (contents_1,
        "Hello all computer users") ;
    strcpy (contents_2, "What a fine day!") ;
    }

void message::display ()
    {
    cout << contents_1 << endl ;
    cout << contents_2 << endl ;
    }
```

```
void main ()
    {
    message hello ;
    hello.initialise () ;
    hello.display () ;
    }
```

3.5.3

(a) The class and the function name.

(b) `Call hello.initialise`

(c) `message::display`
    `Display screen footings`
    `Display contents of message`
    `Display screen headings`

Chapter 4

4.3.1

(a) The ones in the header file have the included file surrounded by < and > which indicates that the file is to be found in the compiler library. The one in the program file has the included file surrounded by quotation marks (") which indicate that the file is to be found in the same directory as the program file.

(b) The `message.h` header file is included in the program file `hello_m.cpp` to allow `hello_m.cpp` to use the facilities described in `message.h`.

4.3.2

(a) The line is included to enable the derived class `any_message` to be derived from the class `message` whose definition is contained in `message.h`.

(b) The keyword `class` starts a new object class definition. `any_message` is the identifier of the new class which is derived from the class `message`. The derivation type `public` allows the facilities of the class `message` to be publicly accessed by the new class.

(c) You declare a data area for a single character by using the keyword (data type) `char` followed by an appropriate identifier.

(d) The `cout` statement does not have an `endl` so that the user-entered message will be appear on the same line of the screen as the prompt.

(e) The first `cin.get` statement gets up to 11 characters from the keyboard and stores them in the area called `contents`. The 12 is to allow for the automatic appending of the end of string character.

(f) The second `cin.get` gets the newline character and stores it in the variable `terminator`. It is necessary because the user must type a newline character to end the message, but the first `cin.get` does not process it.

(g) The `initialise` function is invoked in the program file for the object `do_message` which is of class `any_message`. The declaration of `any_message` has its own member function called `initialise`, hence this is used rather than inheriting the function `initialise` from the class `message`.

4.3.3

The new member data statements should be as follows (note the sizes).

```
char contents_1 [25] ;
char contents_2 [17] ;
```

The statements for the function `initialise` are:

```
strcpy (contents_1, "Hello all computer users") ;
strcpy (contents_2, "What a fine day!") ;
```

The statements for the function `display` are:

```
cout << contents_1 << endl ;
cout << contents_2 << endl ;
```

The program will now produce the correct results without changing the program file `hello_m.cpp`, but the comment in line 2 should be changed to indicate that the program is now displaying two messages.

4.3.4

As the `initialise` function requests a message (of up to 11 characters) from the user and the `display` function displays this message, all that is required is for the two functions to be called again. The following code should be added at the end of the function `main`:

```
do_message.initialise () ;
do_message.display () ;
```

4.3.5

```
forename::initialise
    Declare terminator variable
    Prompt for forename
    Accept forename
    Skip over newline character
```

```
// FORENAME.H
// The object class forename
#include "message.h"
class forename : public message
    {
    public :
        void initialise () ;
    } ;

void forename::initialise ()
    {
    char terminator ;
    cout << "Enter forename: " ;
    cin.get (contents, 12) ;
    cin.get (terminator) ;
    }
```

```
// ASSIGN45.CPP
// A program to display a forename
#include "forename.h"
void main ()
    {
    forename name ;
    name.initialise () ;
    name.display () ;
    }
```

Chapter 5

5.7.1

(a) They could have been written as three separate declarations:
```
int exam_mark ;
int practical_mark ;
int sum ;
```
(b) **float** is the keyword that introduces the declaration of a real number.
(c) The second **#include** statement allows the use of the manipulator **setprecision**.
(d) Eight (plus one for the end of string character).

5.7.2

(a) In this case, we do not need to skip over the newline character because the `cin` statement to obtain **exam_mark** will automatically ignore such a character.

(b) The assignment operator is = (the equals sign).

(c) **const** is used to indicate that the data areas that follow will be assigned a constant (permanent) value that will not change.

(d) The weighted average would be 42.5. The rules for operator precedence means that the multiplication operations are done first, that is 40 * 0.75 (= 30) and 50 * 0.25 (= 12.5); then the addition 30 + 12.5 (= 42.5). An incorrect answer of 20 would be obtained if the operators were executed strictly from left to right, e.g. 40 * 0.75 (= 30); then 30 + 50 (= 80); then 80 * 0.25 (= 20).

5.7.3

(a) The purpose of **sum** is to provide a data area to contain the sum of the two marks. It is not strictly necessary because the computation of the sum need not be a separate statement but could have been done in the `cout` statement in **display_sum** as follows:

```
cout << "The sum of the marks is " <<
        exam_mark + practical_mark << endl ;
```

(b) Three lines are displayed after a blank line as follows.

```
Student identity: EG100 for Module: HIST
Exam mark is 60 Practical mark is 66
The sum of the marks is 126
```

The cursor ends up at the beginning of the next line under the **T** of the word **The**.

(c) It causes the floating point value in **weighted_average** to be output with one decimal place.

5.7.4

Only the data declarations would have to be changed:

```
const float exam_weight = 0.8,
            practical_weight = 0.2 ;
```

5.7.5

```
// MARKS55.H
// The object class student_marks_55
#include "marks.h"
class student_marks_55 : public student_marks
   {
   public :
      void compute_average () ;
      void display_marks_and_average () ;
   protected :
      float average ;
   } ;

void student_marks_55::compute_average ()
   {
   average = sum / 2.0 ;
   }

void student_marks_55::display_marks_and_average ()
   {
   display_marks () ;
   cout << "The average of the marks is "
      << setprecision (1) << average << endl ;
   }
```

```
// ASSIGN55.CPP
// A program to produce the average of a
// student's assessment marks for a subject
#include "marks55.h"
void main ()
   {
   student_marks_55 arithmetic_AB100 ;
   arithmetic_AB100.initialise () ;
   arithmetic_AB100.compute_average () ;
   arithmetic_AB100.display_marks_and_average () ;
   }
```

5.7.6

```
// CIRCLE.H
// The object class circle
#include <iostream.h>
#include <iomanip.h>
class circle
    {
    public :
       void initialise () ;
       void display_area () ;
       void display_circumference () ;
    protected :
       float radius,
             pi ;
    } ;

void circle::initialise ()
    {
    char terminator ;
    pi = 3.1416 ;
    cout <<
       "Enter radius of circle in centimetres " ;
    cin >> radius ;
    cin.get (terminator) ;
    }

void circle::display_area ()
    {
    float area ;
    area = pi * radius * radius ;
    cout << "The area of the circle is "
       << setprecision (2) << area
       << " square cms" << endl ;
    }

void circle::display_circumference ()
    {
    float circumference ;
    circumference = 2 * pi * radius ;
    cout << "The circumference of the circle is "
       << setprecision (2) << circumference
        << " cms" << endl ;
    }
```

```
// ASSIGN56.CPP
// A program to display the area and circumference
// of a circle
#include "circle.h"
void main ()
   {
   circle disk ;
   disk.initialise () ;
   disk.display_area () ;
   disk.display_circumference () ;
   }
```

Chapter 6

6.7.1

(a) A sequence and a selection with no alternative statement specified.

(b) When the marks are not equal.

(c) `Call display_identities`
   `Call display_marks`
   `Display same marks message`
   `Display a blank line`

(d) The operations are indented.

6.7.2

(a) True or false.

(b) The keyword `if`. A relational expression (condition) in parentheses. A statement to be executed if the condition is true.

(c) When **exam_mark** is not the same as **practical_mark** the condition in line 5 is false, hence the statement in line 7 is executed directly.

6.7.3

(a) The keyword `if`. A relational expression (condition) in parentheses. A statement to be executed if the condition is true. The keyword `else`. A statement to be executed if the condition is false.

(b)
```
if (exam_mark >= 70)
   cout << "First class exam mark" << endl ;
if (exam_mark < 70)
   cout << "Not a first class exam mark" << endl ;
```

The code gives the equivalent result but it is not as good as that in figure 6.7. When the first condition is false we know that the exam mark must be less than 70. This means that the **else** part of the code in figure 6.7

does not include `if (exam_mark < 70)`. The second `if` in the above code, however, does need to include this second condition.

(c) The 'greater than or equal to' operator is `>=`.

6.7.4

(a) The second `if` statement is entirely enclosed within the `else` part associated with the first `if`. That is, it is executed only when the first `if` statement's condition is false.

(b)
```
if (exam_mark == practical_mark)
    cout << "The marks are the same" << endl ;
if (exam_mark > practical_mark)
    cout << "Exam mark is better" << endl ;
if (practical mark > exam_mark)
    cout << "Practical mark is better" << endl ;
```

The code is inferior to that in figure 6.11 because all three conditions are mutually exclusive. As in the previous question the final test is unnecessary because 'practical mark better' is the only possible outcome if the first two conditions prove false.

(c) A semicolon is required after each statement to be executed when the condition is true or false, but not after the relational expression.

(d)
```
if (exam_mark == practical_mark)
    cout << "The marks are the same" << endl ;
else
    if (exam_mark > practical_mark)
        cout << "Exam mark is better" << endl ;
    else
        cout << "Practical mark is better" << endl ;
```

6.7.5

(a) A compound statement is a sequence of statements enclosed by braces.

(b) A semicolon is not used after the right brace of a compound statement. So, the only semicolons used are those that separate the individual statements within a compound statement.

(c)

```
void same_mark ()
   {
   cout << "The marks are the same" << endl ;
   cout << "  both are " << exam_mark << endl ;
   }

void exam_better ()
   {
   cout << "The exam mark is better" << endl ;
   cout << "The exam mark is " << exam_mark ;
   cout << " the practical mark is " <<
      practical_mark << endl ;
   }

void practical_better ()
   {
   cout << "The practical mark is better"
      << endl ;
   cout << "The practical mark is " <<
      practical_mark ;
   cout << " the exam mark is " << exam_mark
      << endl ;
   }

void student_marks_1::test_marks ()
   {
   display_identities () ;
   if (exam_mark == practical_mark)
      same_mark () ;
   else if (exam_mark > practical_mark)
      exam_better () ;
   else
      practical_better () ;
   cout << endl ;
   }
```

6.7.6

```
student_marks_1::test_marks
    Call display_identities
    IF exam mark and practical mark over 65
        Display a blank line
        Display exam mark and practical mark
    ELSE IF exam mark over 65
        Display exam mark
    ELSE IF practical mark over 65
        Display practical mark
    Display a blank line
```

6.7.7

```
if (exam_mark < practical_mark)
    {
    cout << "The exam mark is worse" << endl ;
    cout << "The marks are not the same" << endl ;
    }
else if (practical_mark < exam_mark)
    {
    cout << "The practical mark is worse" << endl ;
    cout << "The marks are not the same" << endl ;
    }
```

6.7.8

```
// RECTANG.H
// The object class rectangle
#include <iostream.h>
#include <iomanip.h>
class rectangle
    {
    public :
        void initialise () ;
        void display_area () ;
        void display_perimeter () ;
    protected :
        float length,
              width ;
    } ;
```

```
void rectangle::initialise ()
   {
   char terminator ;
   cout <<
      "Enter length of rectangle in centimetres " ;
   cin >> length ;
   cout <<
      "Enter width of rectangle in centimetres " ;
   cin >> width ;
   cin.get (terminator) ;
   }

void rectangle::display_area ()
   {
   float area ;
   if (width == 0)
      {
      cout << "Rectangle is a square" << endl ;
      area = length * length ;
      }
   else
      area = length * width ;
   cout << "The area is "
      << setprecision (2) << area
      << " square centimetres" << endl ;
   }

void rectangle::display_perimeter ()
   {
   float perimeter ;
   if (width == 0)
      perimeter = 4 * length ;
   else
      perimeter = 2 * length + 2 * width ;
   cout << "The perimeter is "
      << setprecision (2) << perimeter
      << " centimetres" << endl ;
   }
```

```
// ASSIGN68.CPP
// A program to display the area and perimeter of a
// rectangle
#include "rectang.h"
void main ()
   {
   rectangle mouse_mat ;
   mouse_mat.initialise () ;
   mouse_mat.display_area () ;
   mouse_mat.display_perimeter () ;
   }
```

Chapter 7

7.5.1

(a) The three logical operators, in order of precedence, are ! (not) && (and) | | (or).

(b) Only the outermost pair of parentheses are necessary to satisfy the syntax rules of C++. The extra parentheses are used to help clarify the code.

(c) The inequality operator is !=.

(d) The relational expression in the innermost parentheses is evaluated. If it yields true, then the negation operator changes it to false and the statement after the **if** is not executed; if it yields false, the negation operator changes this to true and the statement after the **if** is executed.

7.5.2

```
if ((grade_letter >= 'A') && (grade_letter <= 'E'))
    cout << "We have a valid grade letter" ;
else
    cout << "We have an invalid grade letter" ;
```

7.5.3

(a) **grade_letter** is of type **char**. Any value that can be stored in one byte. This usually means a letter of the alphabet, a single digit or a punctuation character.

(b) An integer value or a character value.

(c) The keyword **case**, followed by a possible value of the **switch** expression, followed by a colon followed by one or more statements to be executed when the expression has the specified value.

(d) A **break** statements stops the execution of further statements within **switch**.

(e) If the value of the **switch** expression is not found in any of the **case** groups, the statements associated with **default** are executed.

(f) Grade B gives "The grade is B Very good".
Grade C gives "The grade is C Pass, but you must try harder".
Grade D gives "The grade is D must try harder".

7.5.4

(a) The expression gives an integer value which represents the most significant digit of the weighted average when rounded to the nearest integer. If the weighted average is 23.2 the resultant value is 2. If the weighted average is 46.5 the resultant value is 4. If the weighted average is 79.5 the resultant value is 8. The corresponding values for `grade_letter` are 'E', 'D' and 'A'.

(b) If the value of the **switch** expression matches the value of such a case group, execution drops down to the next statement. In this example, the assignment of `'A'` to `grade_letter`.

7.5.5

```
// MARKS75.H
// The object class student_marks_75
#include "marks2.h"
class student_marks_75 : public student_marks_2
    {
    public :
        void display_average () ;
    } ;

void student_marks_75::display_average ()
    {
    if (sum != 0)
        cout << "Average mark is " << sum / 2
            << endl ;
    else
        cout << "Sum of marks is zero" << endl ;
    }
```

```
// ASSIGN75.CPP
// A program to display the average of a student's
// marks in a subject
#include "marks75.h"
void main ()
    {
    student_marks_75 biology_WE200 ;
    biology_WE200.initialise () ;
    biology_WE200.test_zeros () ;
    biology_WE200.display_average () ;
    }
```

7.5.6

```
student_marks_76::initialise
   Call student_marks::initialise
   IF both exam mark and practical mark exceed 74
      Set grade letter to 'A'
   ELSE IF exam mark and practical mark exceed 49
      Set grade letter to 'B'
   ELSE
      Set grade letter to 'C'
```

```
// MARKS76.H
// The object class student_marks_76
#include "marks2.h"
class student_marks_76 : public student_marks_2
   {
   public :
      void initialise () ;
   } ;

void student_marks_76::initialise ()
   {
   student_marks::initialise () ;
   if ((exam_mark > 74) && (practical_mark > 74))
      grade_letter = 'A' ;
   else if ((exam_mark > 49) && (practical_mark >
      49))
      grade_letter = 'B' ;
   else
      grade_letter = 'C' ;
   }
```

```
// ASSIGN76.CPP
// A program to display a student's marks and
// grades in a course
#include "marks76.h"
void main ()
   {
   student_marks_76 chemistry_SE300 ;
   chemistry_SE300.initialise () ;
   chemistry_SE300.display_grade () ;
   }
```

7.5.7

```
// CONVERT.H
// The object class convert
#include <iostream.h>
class convert
   {
   public :
      void get_number () ;
      void convert_to_roman_numeral () ;
      void display_roman_numeral () ;
   protected :
      int   number ;
      char roman_numeral ;
   } ;

void convert::get_number ()
   {
   char terminator ;
   cout <<
      "Enter number " ;
   cin >> number ;
   cin.get (terminator) ;
   }

void convert::convert_to_roman_numeral ()
   {
   switch (number)
      {
      case 1    : roman_numeral = 'I' ;
                  break ;
      case 5    : roman_numeral = 'V' ;
                  break ;
      case 10   : roman_numeral = 'X' ;
                  break ;
      case 50   : roman_numeral = 'L' ;
                  break ;
      case 100 : roman_numeral = 'C' ;
                  break ;
      default   : roman_numeral = '?' ;
      }
   }
```

```
void convert::display_roman_numeral ()
    {
    cout << number ;
    if (roman_numeral == '?')
        cout << " cannot be converted" << endl ;
    else
        cout << " gives the Roman numeral " <<
            roman_numeral << endl ;
    }
```

```
// ASSIGN77.CPP
// A program to convert a number to a roman numeral
#include "convert.h"
void main ()
    {
    convert dial ;
    dial.get_number () ;
    dial.convert_to_roman_numeral () ;
    dial.display_roman_numeral () ;
    }
```

Chapter 8

8.5.1

 (a) None at all.

 (b) The `cin.get (terminator)` statement.

 (c) The loop would continue indefinitely adding the first component mark to the total practical mark, increasing the number of marks by 1 and displaying the prompt.

 (d) `no_of_marks` would contain 2.

  `total_practical_mark` would contain 110.

  `component_mark` would contain 999.

 (e) It is necessary to avoid the possibility of attempting to divide by zero which would cause an execution error. `no_of_marks` would be zero if the first value typed was 999.

8.5.2

 (a) The first expression is executed once only.

 (b) The third expression is executed once for each time the statements of the loop are executed, that is, 5 times in this example.

 (c) The second expression of the `for` statement would need the 5 changing to 4.

(d) We do not use the read-ahead technique here because the relational expression used to control the **for** loop does not depend on a special 'end' value being obtained. The number of times we need to go round the loop is predefined, so there is no need for a special 'end' value.

(e) The **for** would be replaced by

```
int question_number = 1 ;
while (question_number <= 5)
```

and

```
++ queston_number ;
```

would be included as the last statement in the compound statement associated with the while.

The code in the example is better. It expresses the count-controlled repetition, **question_number** going from 1 to 5 in steps of 1, more concisely.

(f) The relational expression would need to be **(question_number < 5)** or **(question_number <= 4)**. Note also, that the prompt would ask for exam mark 0 then 1 then 2 and so on.

8.5.3

(a) Because the statements after **do** must be executed before the condition following **while** can be tested for the first time.

(b) The **do-while** loop is necessary in this example to ensure that any mark entered by the user outside the range 0 to 20 is ignored. It provides a simple validation check.

(c)
```
cout << "Enter examination mark no. " <<
     question_number << " " ;
cin >> question_mark ;
while (! ((question_mark >= 0) &&
   (question_number <= 20)))
   {
   cout << "Enter examination mark no. " <<
      question_number << " " ;
   cin >> question_mark ;
   }
```

Having to repeat the code before and inside the while loop makes it inferior to that in figure 8.15.

(d) The second expression of the **for** statement would need the 5 changing to 4. The second condition in the **while** would need the 20 changing to 25.

(e)
```
while ((question_number < 0) ||
   (question_number > 25))
```

8.5.4

```
student_marks_84::get_exam_mark
   Declare variables
   Initialise exam mark (=0)
   Prompt for and get first exam question mark
   WHILE exam question mark not -1
      Add exam question mark to exam mark
      Prompt for and get next exam question mark
   Skip over final newline character

student_marks_84::initialise
   Call get_identities
   Call get_practical_mark
   DO
      Call get_exam_mark
   WHILE exam mark not greater than practical mark
   Call do_calculations
```

```
// MARKS84.H
// The object class student_marks_84
#include "marks2A.h"
class student_marks_84 : public student_marks_2A
   {
   public :
      void initialise () ;
      void get_exam_mark () ;
   } ;

void student_marks_84::get_exam_mark ()
   {
   char terminator ;
   int question_mark ;
   exam_mark = 0 ;
   cout << "Enter first exam mark (or -1 to end) " ;
   cin >> question_mark ;
   while (question_mark != -1)
      {
      exam_mark += question_mark ;
      cout <<
          "Enter next exam mark (or -1 to end) " ;
      cin >> question_mark ;
      }
   cin.get (terminator) ;
   }
```

```
void student_marks_84::initialise ()
   {
   get_identities () ;
   get_practical_mark () ;
   do
      get_exam_mark () ;
   while (exam_mark <= practical_mark) ;
   do_calculations () ;
   }
```

8.5.5

```
// TRIANG.H
// The object class triangle
#include <iostream.h>
#include <iomanip.h>
class triangle
   {
   public :
      void initialise () ;
      void display_area () ;
   private :
      float height,
            base ;
   } ;

void triangle::initialise ()
   {
   char terminator ;
   do
      {
      cout <<
         "Enter height of triangle in centimetres " ;
      cin >> height ;
      }
   while (height < 10.0) ;
   do
      {
      cout <<
        "Enter base of triangle in centimetres " ;
      cin >> base ;
      }
   while (base < 12.5) ;
   cin.get (terminator) ;
   }
```

```
void triangle::display_area ()
   {
   float area ;
   area = height * base / 2 ;
   cout << "The area of the triangle is "
      << setprecision (2) << area
      << " square centimetres" << endl ;
   }
```

```
// ASSIGN85.CPP
// A program to display area of triangle
#include "triang.h"
void main ()
   {
   triangle example ;
   for (int counter = 1 ; counter <= 6 ; ++
      counter)
      {
      example.initialise () ;
      example.display_area () ;
      }
   }
```

Chapter 9

9.8.1

 (a) The result type, the function identifier and the types and order of the parameters must be the same.
 (b) The actual parameters must correspond in terms of order and type.
 (c) The prototype is terminated with a semi-colon. Though not mentioned in the text, it is not mandatory for the parameter identifiers to be included in the prototype.
 (d) A string constant, that is a string value that cannot be changed within the function.
 (e) By using braces.
 (f) It is called a number of times with a different parameter each time so saving repetitive coding.

9.8.2

 (a) A type such as `int` or `float` precedes the function identifier.
 (b) It is used to enhance the prompt by including "first" or "next".
 (c) To transmit the required value as the result of a function.
 (d) The prompt and get must be executed at least once before the mark can be tested. `do-while` is the most appropriate construct in such cases.

(e) It is called twice. Each time in an assignment statement, for example
```
component_mark = get_practical_component_mark
    ("first") ;
```

9.8.3

(a) The formal parameter is regarded as an alias of the actual parameter and hence its value can be changed within the function.

(b) As each successive digit is processed, the previous value of **mark** is multiplied by 10.

(c) The character that has been obtained by **cin.get** is a character in the ASCII set that has values of 48 to 57 for the digits '0' to '9'. We need to do arithmetic with the digits so we subtract 48 to give a correct arithmetic representation. This value is then added to **mark**.

(d) The **return** statement causes a value of 0 or 1, that is an indicator of the validity of the mark, to be returned as the result value of the function call.

(e) In the following assignment statement:
```
valid_mark = get_exam_question_mark
    (question_number, question_mark) ;
```

(f) The **A** would be invalid so the value 0 would be returned as the second parameter with a function result of 0.

(g) The value 0 would be returned as the second parameter, and the function result would return a value of 0 indicating an invalid number.

(h) The second parameter would be given a value of 0 and a function result of 1 would be returned.

9.8.4

(a)
```
void display_sum_integers (int first_number, int
    last_number) ;
void display_sum_integers (int first_number, int
    last_number)
display_sum_integers (10, 28) ;
```

(b)
```
int sum_integers (int first_number, int
    second_number) ;
int sum_integers (int first_number, int
    second_number)
answer = sum_integers (10, 28) ;
```

(c)
```
void sum_integers (int first_number, int
    second_number, int& result) ;
void sum_integers (int first_number, int
    second_number, int& result)
sum_integers (10, 28, answer) ;
```

9.8.5

(a) **item_a** would be changed to have a value of 3 and **item_b** would be changed to have a value of 5. This occurs because call by reference using alias parameters is used.

(b) `item_a` and `item_b` would retain their initial values whatever they were because call by value parameters are used; the original values are not changed.

9.8.6

```
// CALCUL.H
// The object class calculator
#include <iostream.h>
#include <iomanip.h>
class calculator
    {
    public :
        void initialise () ;
        void display_result () ;
    private :
        float get_valid_operand (const char* prompt) ;
        void get_valid_operator (char& character) ;
    protected :
        float operand_1,
               operand_2 ;
        char  arithmetic_operator ;
    } ;

void calculator::initialise ()
    {
    operand_1 = get_valid_operand
        ("Enter first operand ") ;
    operand_2 = get_valid_operand
        ("Enter second operand ") ;
    get_valid_operator (arithmetic_operator) ;
    }

float calculator::get_valid_operand (const char*
    prompt)
    {
    float operand ;
    char  terminator ;
    do
        {
        cout << prompt ;
        cin >> operand ;
        }
    while (operand == 0) ;
    cin.get (terminator) ;
    return operand ;
    }
```

```
void calculator::get_valid_operator (char&
   character)
   {
   char terminator ;
   do
      {
      cout << "Enter the operator " ;
      cin.get (character) ;
      cin.get (terminator) ;
      }
   while (! ((character == '+') ||
      (character == '-') || (character == '*')
      || (character == '/'))) ;
   }

void calculator::display_result ()
   {
   float result ;
   switch (arithmetic_operator)
      {
      case '+' : result = operand_1 + operand_2 ;
                 break ;
      case '-' : result = operand_1 - operand_2 ;
                 break ;
      case '*' : result = operand_1 * operand_2 ;
                 break ;
      case '/' : result = operand_1 / operand_2 ;
                 break ;
      }
   cout << operand_1 << " " << arithmetic_operator
      << " " << operand_2 << " = "
      << setprecision (2) << result << endl ;
   }
```

```
// ASSIGN96.CPP
// Implements a simple calculator
#include "calcul.h"
void main ()
   {
   calculator example ;
   example.initialise () ;
   example.display_result () ;
   }
```

Chapter 10

10.4.1

    (a) To reserve memory for an instance of an object and to perform initialisation when an object is created.

    (b) There is no result type for a constructor and a constructor has the same identifier as the object class.

    (c) An instance of the object class `student_marks_2Ba` called `geography_JP100` is created, then the `initialise` function is called.

10.4.2

    (a) After the usual type and identifier, we use an equals sign followed by a value of the appropriate type.

    (b) An instance of the object class `student_marks_2Bb` called `geography_MK110` is created , then

            `Module GEOG    Student MK110`

    is displayed, then the data members `module_identity` and `student_identity` are initialised with the values `GEOG` and `MK110` respectively, then `get_exam_mark`, `get_practical_mark` and `do_calculations` are called.

    (c) An instance of the object class `student_marks_2Bb` called `maths_JP100` is created , then

            `Module MATHS    Student JP100"`

    is displayed, then the data members `module_identity` and `student_identity` are initialised with the values `MATHS` and `JP100` respectively, then the functions `get_exam_mark`, `get_practical_mark` and `do_calculations` are called.

10.4.3

    In figure 10.1, the only change necessary is to include the following two function calls after the call to `initialise` in the constructor `student_marks_2Ba`.

```
display_sum () ;
display_weighted_average () ;
```

    In figure 10.2, remove the calls to the function `display_sum`.

10.4.4

```
// CUBE.H
// The object class cube
#include <iostream.h>
#include <iomanip.h>
#include <math.h>
class cube
    {
    public :
        cube (float length) ;
        void display_volume () ;
        void display_surface_area () ;
    protected :
        float length_of_side ;
    } ;

cube::cube (float length)
    {
    length_of_side = length ;
    display_volume () ;
    display_surface_area () ;
    }

void cube::display_volume ()
    {
    float volume ;
    volume = pow (length_of_side, 3) ;
    cout << "The volume of the cube is "
        << setprecision (2) << volume
        << " cubic centimetres" << endl ;
    }

void cube::display_surface_area ()
    {
    float area ;
    area = pow (length_of_side, 2) * 6 ;
    cout << "The surface area of the cube is "
        << setprecision (2)  << area
        << " square centimetres" << endl ;
    }
```

```
// ASSIG104.CPP
// A program to display area and volume of 2 cubes
#include "cube.h"
void main ()
   {
   cube die (5.5) ;
   cube oxo (1.2) ;
   }
```

Chapter 11

11.3.1

    (a) We need to access the data twice. Once in computing the total (and hence the average), then again when comparing each mark against the average.

    (b) The data type of each element, the identifier and the number of elements.

    (c) The array identifier and the index value of the element required.

    (d) In both cases the number of iterations is known before entering the loop.

    (e) 0 to 11 inclusive.

    (f) The `cout` in `get_marks` would be changed to:
```
cout << "Enter a mark for student no. "
   << student_index + 1 << " : " ;
```
       The second `cout` in `display_marks` would be changed to:
```
cout << "No. " << student_index + 1 << "    "
   << marks [student_index] << endl ;
```

11.3.2

    (a) A mark might not be entered for some students. So not every element of the array will necessarily be given a value from the keyboard. We need to specify a default value for such elements.

    (b) The `while` loop is used here because we do not know at the outset the number of iterations required.

    (c) If a student number of 13 was entered, this would be used as an array index value and would cause unpredictable results or a run-time error because it is outside the range declared for the array.

    (d) A counter, `marks_count` say, would need to be declared and initialised to zero at the beginning of `get_marks`. Then for each mark stored in the array the `marks_count` would be increased by 1. The average mark would be computed by dividing `total` by the `marks_count`.

(e) Not all elements have to be entered (so a default value may be given when initialising the array). The values do not need to be entered in any specific order.

11.3.3

(a) The only change we need to make is to change **no_of_marks** in the **const** declaration to 18.

(b) We change the name of the protected data member **average_mark** to **highest_mark** then compute a value for it by changing **get_marks** to:

```
char terminator ;
highest_mark = 0 ;
for (int student_index = 0 ; student_index <
    no_of_marks ; ++ student_index)
    {
    cout << "Enter a mark for student no. "
        << student_index << " : " ;
    cin >> marks [student_index] ;
    if (marks [student_index] > highest_mark)
        highest_mark = marks [student_index] ;
    }
cin.get (terminator) ;
```

Then use **highest_mark** by changing the **if** statement in **display_marks** to:

```
if (marks [student_index] = highest_mark)
    cout << "No. " << student_index << "   "
        << marks [student_index] << endl ;
```

11.3.4

Include the prototype

```
    void get_a_mark (int& student_no, int& a_mark) ;
```

in the class definition. Define the function **get_a_mark**.

```
    void get_a_mark (int& student_no, int& a_mark)
        {
        do
            {
            cout << Enter student no. and mark: " ;
            cin >> student_no >> a_mark ;
            }
        while (((student_no < 0) || (student_no >=
            no_of_marks)) && (student_no != 999)) ;
        }
```

Note that an alternative form of the condition is

```
while (! ((student_no >= 0) && (student_no <
    no_of_marks) || (student_no = 999)))
```

Replace the **cout** followed by the **cin** in **get_marks** with

```
get_a_mark (student_number, mark) ;
```

11.3.5

```
// SALES.H
// The object class sales
#include <iostream.h>
   const int no_of_sales = 20 ;
class sales
   {
   public :
      void get_sales () ;
      void display_best () ;
   protected :
      float sales_figures [no_of_sales] ;
      float best_sales_figure ;
   } ;

void sales::get_sales ()
   {
   char terminator ;
   best_sales_figure = 0 ;
   for (int sales_index = 0 ; sales_index <
      no_of_sales ; ++ sales_index)
      {
      cout <<
         "Enter sales figure for sales person " <<
         sales_index + 10 << ": " ;
      cin >> sales_figures [sales_index] ;
      if (sales_figures [sales_index] >
         best_sales_figure)
         best_sales_figure = sales_figures
            [sales_index] ;
      }
   cin.get (terminator) ;
   }
```

```
void sales::display_best ()
   {
   int count = 0 ;
   for (int sales_index = 0 ; sales_index <
      no_of_sales ; ++ sales_index)
      {
      if (sales_figures [sales_index] >=
         best_sales_figure * 0.8)
         {
         cout << "Sales person " << sales_index +
            10 << " achieved target" << endl ;
         ++ count ;
         }
      }
   cout << count <<
      " sales persons achieved target" << endl ;
   }
```

```
// ASSIG115.CPP
// A program to get sales figures for 20 sales
// people and display those that achieved target
#include "sales.h"
void main ()
   {
   sales year_1997 ;
   year_1997.get_sales () ;
   year_1997.display_best () ;
   }
```

Chapter 12

12.3.1

   (a) The member data **exam_mark** and **student_identity** are declared
       as **protected** in their original definition, which means they can only
       be accessed by objects in which they are declared (the base class) or
       objects of a derived class. In this example we need to access them in the
       object class **module_A**.
   (b) The result type of **return_student_mark** is int. The result type of
       return_student_identity is char* (a pointer to an item of type
       char).
   (c) The function **initialise**. It is inherited from the object class
       student_marks_2B.

12.3.2

(a) The type of each element is the object class **student_marks_2Bc**, the array identifier is **mark_table**, and the array size is the constant **no_of_marks**.

(b) The function **initialise** is called 12 times, once for each object in the array **mark_table**. When it is called, the member data for the object are given initial values by calls to the functions **get_identities**, **get_exam_mark**, **get_practical_mark**, and **do_calculations**.

(c) The function **return_exam_mark** is invoked to store the exam mark for the **mark_table [student_index]** in **mark**. The variable **mark** is then used twice in the following **if** statement. The function could have been used directly in the **if** statement, but this would have meant invoking it twice which would incur a small increase in execution time. This advantage is partly offset by the disadvantage of using an extra variable which incurs a small increase in memory requirements.

(d) The inheritance hierarchy that includes **student_marks_2Bc** as a derived class of **student_marks_2B** is an example of inheritance. The array of objects of type **student_marks_2Bc** found in the object class **module_A** is an example of aggregation.

12.3.3

```cpp
// PERSON.H
// The object class person
#include <iostream.h>
class person
    {
    public :
        void display () ;
        void initialise () ;
    protected :
        char surname [15] ;
    } ;

void person::display ()
    {
    cout << surname << endl ;
    }
```

```
void person::initialise ()
   {
   char terminator ;
   cout << "Enter surname: " ;
   cin.get (surname, 15) ;
   cin.get (terminator) ;
   }
```

```
// MEMBERS.H
// The object class members
#include "person.h"
   const int no_of_members = 10 ;
class members
   {
   protected :
      person person_list [no_of_members] ;
   public :
      void get_names () ;
      void display_names () ;
   } ;

void members::get_names ()
   {
   for (int person_index = 0 ; person_index <
      no_of_members ; ++ person_index)
      {
      person_list [person_index].initialise () ;
      }
   }

void members::display_names ()
   {
   cout << endl << "Membership in reverse order"
      << endl ;
   for (int person_index = no_of_members - 1 ;
      person_index >= 0; -- person_index)
      {
      person_list [person_index].display () ;
      }
   }
```

```
// ASSIG123.CPP
// A program to get a list of names and
// display it in the reverse order
#include "members.h"
void main ()
    {
    members club ;
    club.get_names () ;
    club.display_names () ;
    }
```

Chapter 13

13.3.1

(a) We use a two dimensional array because it is easier to think of the data in terms of rows (module data) and columns (student data) rather than a list.

(b)

module index	student index
0	0
0	1
0	2
0	3
0	4
0	5
1	0
1	1
1	2
1	3
1	4
1	5
2	0
2	1
2	2
2	3
2	4
2	5
3	0
3	1
3	2
3	3
3	4
3	5

(c) This manipulator ensures that the displayed numerical data is properly tabulated. Its function is to set a field width for the next item of data to be displayed. All items will have the same field width regardless of value by right-justifying the data and adding leading spaces as necessary.

(d) We might attempt to access an array element with, say, index values of [5] [3] which is illegal because the maximum index value allowed for the first index in the array's declaration is 3. Unpredictable results or a run-time error would occur.

13.3.2

(a) We use **for** loops because we know at the outset the number of iterations required. It is convenient to use two **for** loops nested because we can process each row by the outer loop and each element within that row by the inner loop.

(b) In this case there would be no difference other than the order in which the array elements are set to zero. In other cases, for example when accepting data from the keyboard, this would be more significant because it would affect the order in which the data are to be entered.

13.3.3

Declare an array initialised to zero.
```
int student_totals [no_of_students] = {0} ;
```

Add the following line after the code to add to **module_total**.
```
student_totals [student_index] += marks
                [module_index][student_index] ;
```

Add the following code at the end of the function.
```
cout << "   Averages   " ;
for (int student_index = 0 ; student_index <
    no_of_students ; ++ student_index)
    cout << setw (4) << student_totals
        [student_index] / no_of_modules ;
cout << endl ;
```

13.3.4

```cpp
// ANIMALS.H
// The object class animals
#include <iostream.h>
#include <iomanip.h>
   const int no_of_weights = 20 ;
   const int no_of_ages = 10 ;
class animals
   {
   public :
      animals () ;
      void get_age_and_weight (int& the_age,
         int& the_weight) ;
      void display_table () ;
   protected :
      int table [no_of_weights] [no_of_ages] ;
   } ;

animals::animals ()
   {
   char terminator ;
   int weight,
       age ;
   for (int weight_counter = 0 ; weight_counter <
      no_of_weights ; ++ weight_counter)
      for (int age_counter = 0 ; age_counter <
         no_of_ages ; ++ age_counter)
         table [weight_counter] [age_counter] = 0 ;
   get_age_and_weight (age, weight) ;
   while (age != 999)
      {
      ++ table [weight - 20] [age - 5] ;
      get_age_and_weight (age, weight) ;
      }
   cin.get (terminator) ;
   }
```

```
void animals::get_age_and_weight (int& the_age,
   int& the_weight)
   {
   do
      {
      cout << "Enter age then weight: " ;
      cin >> the_age >> the_weight ;
      }
   while ((the_age > 14) && (the_age < 5) &&
      (the_weight > 39) && (the_weight < 20)
      && (the_age != 999)) ;
   }

void animals::display_table ()
   {
   cout << "          5yrs   6yrs   7yrs   8yrs   "
      << "9yrs 10yrs 11yrs 12yrs 13yrs 14yrs"
      << endl ;
   for (int weight_index = 0 ; weight_index <
      no_of_weights ; ++ weight_index)
      {
      cout << weight_index + 20 << "kgs" ;
      for (int age_index = 0 ; age_index <
         no_of_ages ; ++ age_index)
         {
         cout << setw (6) << table [weight_index]
            [age_index] ;
         }
      cout << endl ;
      }
   }
```

```
// ASSIG134.CPP
// A program to display the number of animals with
// each possible combination of weight and age
#include "animals.h"
void main ()
   {
   animals cats,
           dogs ;
   cats.display_table () ;
   dogs.display_table () ;
   }
```

Chapter 14

14.6.1

(a) **module_total** is local to the function **display_marks**; its scope is the whole of that function. **student_index** is local to the braces immediately outside its declaration (lines 6 and 15 of the function).

(b) **no_of_modules** and **no_of_students** are global constants. Their scope is the entire **course.h** file and any file that includes it.
The array **marks** is global, it may be used in the header file or any file that includes it, but being protected it may only be used within functions of the object class **course** or any derived classes.

(c) A **static** variable is initialised only once. Its value is retained when it goes out of scope.

14.6.2

(a) The object **history_MK350** has global scope. Its lifetime is the duration of the execution of the whole of the program.

(b) The automatic object **english_JP200** has local scope. Its lifetime is during a single execution of the body of the **for** statement.

(c) While both **english_JP200** and **french_EP100** are local in scope, **english_JP200** is automatic while **french_EP100** is static. The execution of **display_identities** and **display_marks** for the object **english_JP200** will relate to a new object each time the functions are called (that is, each time round the loop). The execution of these functions for **french_EP100** will relate to the same object each time they are called.

14.6.3

(a) The type is followed by an asterisk. Initialisation is normally to a null value represented by the constant **NULL**.

(b) The function **malloc** obtains memory of a specified size from the memory management system and returns the address of the memory obtained as a pointer.

(c) If **malloc** is unable to obtain sufficient memory a null value is returned. This is tested to ensure that the program does not proceed when memory is not available.

(d) When **int_pointer** is used, a memory address is given. When ***int_pointer** is used, it dereferences the variable so that the contents of the memory whose address is in **int_pointer** is given.

14.6.4

(a) In the same way as any variable. We follow the type (class name) with an asterisk.

(b) A programmer-declared destructor is defined in the same way as a constructor except that the identifier is preceded by ~ (tilde) and there are no arguments.

(c) The constructor is used to initialise **student_index** to -1 and each element of **student**, the array of pointers, to a null value.

(d) The destructor is necessary so that the memory obtained for dynamic objects is released back to the memory management system.

(e) The **delete** operator returns the memory of the object whose address is given.

14.6.5

(a) The **new** operator allocates memory for an object and the address of the memory is then stored in an element of the array, which is an object pointer variable.

(b) The arrow operator (**->**) is used to access a particular member of an object's class indirectly through a pointer to the object.

(c) The first statement simply displays a message. The second statement calls the function **display_identities**, inherited by the class **student_marks_2B**, for the object pointed to by the element of the array **student** indexed by **student_index**. The third statement returns the memory of the object whose address is contained in the currently indexed array element. The fourth statement sets the value of that element to **NULL**. The fifth statement decreases **student_index** by 1 to maintain an accurate count of the objects currently in use.

14.6.6

(a) The following two statements should be included in **get_student** immediately before the call to **display_marks**.

```
cout << "Student added" ;
student [student_index]->display_identities () ;
```

(b) The function **remove_student** should be revised as follows.

```
void module_B::remove_student ()
    {
    if (student [0] != NULL)
        {
        cout << "Student removed" ;
        student [0]->display_identities () ;
        delete student [0] ;
        for (int counter = 1 ; counter <=
            student_index ; ++ counter)
            {
            student [counter - 1] = student [counter] ;
            }
        student [student_index] = NULL ;
        -- student_index ;
        }
    else
        cout << "No students left" << endl ;
    }
```

14.6.7

```
// CAR.H
// The object class car
#include <iostream.h>
class car
    {
    public :
        car () ;
        void display_details () ;
        char* return_registration () ;
    protected :
        char model [16] ;
        char registration [8] ;
    } ;

car::car ()
    {
    char terminator ;
    cout << "Enter model name " ;
    cin.get (model, 16) ;
    cin.get (terminator) ;
    cout << "Enter registration " ;
    cin.get (registration, 8) ;
    cin.get (terminator) ;
    }
```

```
void car::display_details ()
   {
   cout << "Model " << model << " Registration "
      << registration << endl ;
   }

char* car::return_registration ()
   {
   return registration ;
   }
```

```
// CARSALES.H
// The object class car_sales
#include <stdlib.h>
#include <string.h>
#include "car.h"
const int maximum_cars = 10 ;
class car_sales
   {
   protected :
      car* cars_in_stock [maximum_cars] ;
   public :
      car_sales () ;
      ~car_sales () ;
      void sell_car () ;
   } ;

car_sales::car_sales ()
   {
   for (int counter = 0 ; counter < maximum_cars ;
      ++ counter)
      {
      cars_in_stock [counter] = new car ;
      if (cars_in_stock [counter] == NULL)
         {
         cout << "No memory available" << endl ;
         exit (1) ;
         }
      }
   }
```

```cpp
car_sales::~car_sales ()
   {
   cout << "Cars left in stock" << endl ;
   for (int counter = 0 ; counter < maximum_cars ;
      ++ counter)
      {
      if (cars_in_stock [counter] != NULL)
         {
         cars_in_stock [counter]->
            display_details () ;
         delete cars_in_stock [counter] ;
         }
      }
   }

void car_sales::sell_car ()
   {
   char this_registration [8] ;
   char terminator ;
   cout << "Enter registration of car to be sold " ;
   cin.get (this_registration, 8) ;
   cin.get (terminator) ;
   int car_index = 0,
       found = 0 ;
   while (! ((found) || (car_index ==
      maximum_cars)))
      {
      if (cars_in_stock [car_index] != NULL)
         {
         if (! strcmp (cars_in_stock [car_index]->
            return_registration (),
            this_registration))
            {
            found = 1 ;
            cout << "Car sold " << this_registration
               << endl ;
            delete cars_in_stock [car_index] ;
            cars_in_stock [car_index] = NULL ;
            }
         }
      ++ car_index ;
      }
   if (! found)
      cout << "Car not found" << endl ;
   }
```

```
// ASSIG147.CPP
// A simple car sales program
#include "carsales.h"
void main ()
   {
   car_sales ford ;
   char option,
        terminator ;
   do
      {
      cout << "Enter option: 'S' sell a car"
         << endl ;
      cout << "                'E' end this run"
         << endl ;
      cout << "Enter option: " ;
      cin.get (option) ;
      cin.get (terminator) ;
      if (option == 'S')
         ford.sell_car () ;
      }
   while (option != 'E') ;
   }
```

Chapter 15

15.5.1

(a) The components of a serial disk file exist in creation order, whereas the components of a sequential file have been sorted into some order based on the values contained in key fields.

(b) `cin >> character` will skip past white-space characters; to read such characters, `cin.get (character)` should be used.

(c) `cin >> message` will skip past white-space characters then transfer characters to `message` up to the first white-space character; if the message could contain spaces then `cin.get (message, 12)` should be used to transfer up to 11 characters terminated by the newline character.

15.5.2

(a) You can use

```
ofstream object_name ("filename.ext") ;
```

or

```
ofstream object_name ;
object_name.open ("filename.ext") ;
```

(b) An opening mode is an integer value (or constant) that represents a way in which a file stream may be opened.

(c) At the point in which it is executed, the stream object `output_file` falls out of scope due to the function finishing. When this happens the object's destructor is called which includes a `close` function call.

(d) The only difference to the programmer is that the disk file stream is associated with an identifier of type `ofstream` (or `ifstream`) as opposed to the pre-declared object `cout`.

(e) It is used as a separator between the exam mark and the student identity. It would not be necessary if the first character of the student identity was always a non-numeric character because the read operation for the exam mark would terminate correctly upon recognising the first character of the student identity.

15.5.3

(a) The technique is necessary because the end of input stream state is only set when we have already read the last item in the file and another attempt to read from it is made.

(b) The technique will allow files of any length, even zero-length (empty) files, to be processed.

(c) You can use

```
ifstream object_name ("filename.ext") ;
```
or
```
ifstream object_name ;
object_name.open ("filename.ext") ;
```

(d) The file to be used in an input stream may not exist or may not be available to the program.

(e) We use the `eof` function of the object class `ifstream`; `input_file.eof()` returns the value true.

15.5.4

(a) There may be many disk files used in a program, but only one keyboard and monitor screen. There are a number of different ways in which we may organise data in disk files. When we have finished with a file it should be closed so that it can be re-used in other programs.

(b) A persistent object exists between program runs. It must normally be implemented using some form of disk storage.

(c) An array uses memory that is allocated for the duration of a program run. Its contents are lost when the program finishes.

15.5.5

```
// MODULE_C.H
// The object class module_C (amended)
#include <fstream.h>
#include <stdlib.h>
#include "marks2bc.h"
class module_C
   {
   public :
      void write_students () ;
      void read_students () ;
   protected :
      student_marks_2Bc* student ;
   } ;
```

```
void module_C::write_students ()
   {
   ofstream output_file ("student.dat") ;
   char repeat_character,
        terminator ;
   do
      {
      student = new student_marks_2Bc ;
      if (student == NULL)
         {
         cout << "No memory available" << endl ;
         exit (1) ;
         }
      student->initialise () ;
      output_file << student->return_exam_mark ()
         << ' ' << student->return_practical_mark ()
         << ' ' << student->return_student_identity
         () << endl ;
      delete student ;
      cout << "Press A for another, E to end " ;
      cin.get (repeat_character) ;
      cin.get (terminator) ;
      }
   while (repeat_character == 'A') ;
   output_file.close () ;
   }
```

```cpp
void module_C::read_students ()
   {
   char identity [9] ;
   int  exam_mark,
        practical_mark ;
   char separator ;
   ifstream input_file ("student.dat") ;
   if (! input_file)
      {
      cout << "Student file not available" << endl ;
      exit (1) ;
      }
   input_file >> exam_mark ;
   cout << endl << "Students with merits" << endl ;
   while (! input_file.eof())
      {
      input_file >> practical_mark ;
      input_file.get (separator) ;
      input_file.get (identity, 9) ;
      if ((exam_mark > 50) && (practical_mark > 50))
         cout << "Student " << identity << "\t"
              << setw (3) << exam_mark << "\t"
              << setw (3) << practical_mark << endl ;
      input_file >> exam_mark ;
      }
   input_file.close () ;
   }
```

15.5.6

```cpp
// AGES.H
// The object class ages
#include <fstream.h>
#include <iostream.h>
#include <stdlib.h>
#include <iomanip.h>
class ages
   {
   public :
      void get_ages_and_frequencies () ;
      void display_table () ;
      void set_maximum_age (int given_age) ;
   protected :
      int maximum_age ;
   } ;
```

```
void ages::get_ages_and_frequencies ()
   {
   ofstream output_file ("ages.dat") ;
   int age,
       frequency ;
   for (age = 1 ; age <= 25 ; ++ age)
      {
      cout << "Enter frequency for age " << age
         << ' ' ;
      cin >> frequency ;
      if (frequency != 0)
         output_file << age << ' ' << frequency
            << endl ;
      }
   output_file.close () ;
}
```

```
void ages::display_table ()
   {
   int age,
       frequency ;
   cout << endl << "TABLE OF ACCIDENT FREQUENCIES "
      << "BY AGE UP TO AGE " << maximum_age
      << endl << endl ;
   ifstream input_file ("ages.dat") ;
   if (! input_file)
      {
      cout << "Ages file not available" << endl ;
      exit (1) ;
      }
   input_file >> age ;
   while ((! input_file.eof()) &&
      (age <= maximum_age))
      {
      input_file >> frequency ;
      cout << "   " << setw (2) << age << " years"
         << "\t" << setw (4) << frequency << endl ;
      input_file >> age ;
      }
   input_file.close () ;
   }
```

```
void ages::set_maximum_age (int given_age)
   {
   maximum_age = given_age ;
   }
```

```
// ASSIG156.CPP
// A program to get accident frequencies for all
// ages and display a table up to age 21
#include "ages.h"
void main ()
   {
   ages horses ;
   horses.get_ages_and_frequencies () ;
   horses.set_maximum_age (21) ;
   horses.display_table () ;
   }
```

```
// ASSIG157.CPP
// A program to read the file ages.dat
// and display a table up to age 15
#include "ages.h"
void main ()
   {
   ages horses ;
   horses.set_maximum_age (15) ;
   horses.display_table () ;
   }
```

Chapter 16

16.6.1

(a) It is overloaded in the sense that, although it retains the same meaning, it does different jobs depending on the context in which it is used. For example, it may be used to perform integer arithmetic or real arithmetic.

(b) Coercion is the automatic conversion of an expression to a different form to enable arithmetic to be performed on it.

(c) A type cast is a means of imposing the conversion of a value to another type. We may use it whenever a conversion from one type to another is required (and there is no coercion), such as converting a float value to an integer.

(d) The assignment operator allows the assignment of different data types, so that it may be used to make a copy of a complete object.

16.6.2

(a) The keyword `friend` is used to denote that it may have access to the data members of `student_marks_2Bd` objects. The result type is `int`. The identifier in the prototype is the keyword `operator` followed by the operator `>`. Finally the types of the parameters to be used are as usual specified in parentheses: two objects of the class `student_marks_2Bd`.

(b) A friend function must be declared as `friend` in the object class it wishes to have access to. It is not part of that object class.

(c)
```
if ((student_1.practical_mark >
    student_2.practical_mark) &&
    (student_1.exam_mark != 0))
    return 1 ;
else
    return 0 ;
```

16.6.3

(a) `Character output: B`

(b) They each have a different signature: a different type for the parameter. Hence, for example, a function call with an actual parameter of the type `int` will call the version of display with the formal parameter of the type `int`.

16.6.4

(a) They each have a different signature: one has a parameter, the other does not. So, an object instantiation with an actual parameter will call the constructor with the parameter, an object instantiation with no actual parameter will call the constructor without a parameter.

(b) The object `excellent_student` would be created and the second constructor would be called. This would initialise the data member `exam_mark` to 100.

16.6.5

(a) The keyword `template` is followed by the template's parameter in angular brackets, in this case the class `T`. Then there is the function result type: the class `T`, followed by the function identifier `greater`. This is followed by the function's formal parameters in parentheses, in this case two items of class `T`, `first` and `second`.

(b) The operator `>` must be defined by the compiler or as an operator function.

16.6.6

We change the header file `marks2bd.h` by replacing the operator function `operator >` with the new operator function `operator <`.

```
. . .
     friend int operator < (student_marks_2Bd
       student_a, student_marks_2Bd student_b) ;
. . .
. . .
int operator < (student_marks_2Bd student_a,
   student_marks_2Bd student_b)
   {
   if (student_a.practical_mark <
      student_b.practical_mark)
      return 1 ;
   else
      return 0 ;
   }
```

We change the program file **top_stud.cpp** so that all references to
best_student are replaced by **worst_student**. We change the
relational operator of the **if** statement from > to <. Finally, we change
the text of the **cout** statement.

16.6.7

In **examp16a.h**, we declare the member function
   void display (char a_char, int a_int,
      float a_real) ;
for the class **examp16a**, then include the definition

```
void examp16a::display(char a_char, int a_int,
   float a_real)
   {
   display (a_char) ;
   display (a_int) ;
   display (a_real) ;
   }
```

In **overload.cpp**, we add the statement

   example.display (letter, integer_number,
      real_number) ;

16.6.8

```
// TEMP168.H
// A template for functions to return the highest
// value of three items
template <class T> T greatest (T first, T second,
   T third)
   {
   if ((first > second) && (first > third))
      return first ;
   else if (second > third)
      return second ;
   else
      return third ;
   }
```

```
// ASSIG168.CPP
// A program to display the highest value of three
// integers and the best of three students
#include "temp168.h"
#include "marks2be.h"
void main ()
   {
   int first_integer,
       second_integer,
       third_integer ;
   char terminator ;
   cout << "Please enter three integer values: " ;
   cin >> first_integer >> second_integer >>
      third_integer ;
   cin.get (terminator) ;
   cout << "Greatest of the three integers is " <<
      greatest (first_integer, second_integer,
      third_integer) << endl ;
   student_marks_2Be first_student,
                     second_student,
                     third_student ;
   cout << endl << "Best student is:" ;
   greatest (first_student, second_student,
      third_student).display_identities () ;
   }
```

Appendix C : C++ Keywords and Operators

C.1 Keywords

asm	auto	break	case
catch	char	class	const
continue	default	delete	do
double	else	enum	extern
float	for	friend	goto
if	inline	int	long
new	operator	private	protected
public	register	return	short
signed	sizeof	static	struct
switch	template	this	throw
try	typedef	union	unsigned
virtual	void	volatile	while

C.2 Operators

Precedence	Operator	Meaning
1	::	scope resolution
2=	.	member access
2=	->	member access
2=	[]	subscripting
2=	()	function call
2=	()	grouping
2=	sizeof	size of item
3=	++	incrementation
3=	--	decrementation
3=	!	not
3=	-	unary minus
3=	+	unary plus
3=	&	address
3=	*	dereferencing
3=	new	allocate
3=	delete	deallocate
3=	()	type cast
4=	*	multiply
4=	/	divide
4=	%	give remainder
5=	+	addition
5=	-	subtraction
6=	<<	insertion (and shift left)
6=	>>	extraction (and shift right)
7=	<	less than
7=	<=	less than or equal to
7=	>	greater than
7=	>=	greater than or equal to
8=	==	equal to
8=	!=	not equal to
9	&&	logical and
10	||	logical or
11=	=	assignment
11=	*=	multiply and assignment
11=	/=	divide and assignment
11=	%=	give remainder and assignment
11=	+=	add and assignment
11=	-=	subtract and assignment
12	,	comma

Appendix D : The ASCII Character Set

0	nul	32	space	64	@	96	`
1	soh	33	!	65	A	97	a
2	stx	34	"	66	B	98	b
3	etx	35	#	67	C	99	c
4	eot	36	$	68	D	100	d
5	enq	37	%	69	E	101	e
6	ack	38	&	70	F	102	f
7	bel	39	'	71	G	103	g
8	bs	40	(	72	H	104	h
9	ht	41	)	73	I	105	i
10	lf	42	*	74	J	106	j
11	vt	43	+	75	K	107	k
12	ff	44	,	76	L	108	l
13	cr	45	-	77	M	109	m
14	so	46	.	78	N	110	n
15	si	47	/	79	O	111	o
16	dle	48	0	80	P	112	p
17	dcl	49	1	81	Q	113	q
18	dc2	50	2	82	R	114	r
19	dc3	51	3	83	S	115	s
20	dc4	52	4	84	T	116	t
21	nak	53	5	85	U	117	u
22	syn	54	6	86	V	118	v
23	etb	55	7	87	W	119	w
24	can	56	8	88	X	120	x
25	em	57	9	89	Y	121	y
26	sub	58	:	90	Z	122	z
27	esc	59	;	91	[	123	{
28	fs	60	<	92	\	124		
29	gs	61	=	93	]	125	}
30	rs	62	>	94	^	126	~
31	us	63	?	95	—	127	del

The characters with values 0 to 31 and 127 are special (control) characters of no general concern to the novice programmer. They are given for completeness.

Index